Start-Ups DECLASSIFIED

Start-Ups DECLASSIFIED

An Insider's Playbook for Success

Stephen J. Andriole

BEP

BUSINESS EXPERT PRESS

Leader in applied, concise business books

Start-Ups DECLASSIFIED: An Insider's Playbook for Success

Copyright © Business Expert Press, LLC, 2025

Cover design by Stephen Andriole

Interior design by Exeter Premedia Services Private Ltd., Chennai, India

First published in 2025 by
Business Expert Press, LLC
222 East 46th Street, New York, NY 10017
www.businessexpertpress.com

ISBN-13: 978-1-63742-804-7 (paperback)
ISBN-13: 978-1-63742-805-4 (e-book)

Business Expert Press Entrepreneurship and Small Business Management Collection

First edition: 2025

10 9 8 7 6 5 4 3 2 1

EU SAFETY REPRESENTATIVE
Mare Nostrum Group B.V.
Mauritskade 21D
1091 GC Amsterdam
The Netherlands
gpsr@mare-nostrum.co.uk

Description

You're an entrepreneur and should already be thinking about how to get rich—filthy rich—before you write one line of code or define the service you plan to offer. If you die, you die. But you should not die without dreaming about a house in the Hamptons and a private jet. This is why you never sleep.

Start-Ups DECLASSIFIED can help. It's a must read because it describes the real start-up process based on actual cases—not *theories* about how to create, grow, or exit startups. The book offers lessons learned for every step of the start-up process, ranging from ideation to fundraising to scaling to exiting—as well as a real description of how the sometimes-audacious cast of characters actually behaves. Every lesson is grounded in experience. It's a practical book full of insider analyses, observations, and lessons from start-up cases where the author was *in the room*.

This book describes the real start-up process—not the one described by pundits or the uninitiated—followed by the steps necessary to cut through the articles, books, and TED talks about how to *do* startups. *Start-Ups DECLASSIFIED* is a playbook for entrepreneurs.

Start-Ups DECLASSIFIED says the quiet things out loud. The book is about increasing the probability of success. It leapfrogs the nonsense that permeates start-up myths and movies. If you're a serious entrepreneur, you will love this book.

Contents

Foreword

The world of entrepreneurship is not for the faint of heart. With nearly 90% of start-ups failing, the dream of building something extraordinary—something that disrupts industries or changes lives—is fraught with challenges.

Steve Andriole's *Start-Ups DECLASSIFIED* is a beacon in this daunting landscape. It provides a candid, unvarnished account of what it truly takes to succeed and frankly demystifies the start-up journey. Steve's consummate expertise, combined with his personal experiences—his "lessons from the trenches," as he calls them—adds depth and authenticity to this guide, making this book essential reading for aspiring entrepreneurs, seasoned founders and investors alike.

Steve Andriole is not just a theorist; he's a practitioner who has lived the start-up journey from almost every conceivable angle. From his groundbreaking work at DARPA, where he pioneered predictive analytics and the defense applications of AI, to his leadership roles in academia and corporate America, and his involvement with venture capital during the dot.com boom, Steve's career reflects a deep understanding of the innovation ecosystem. His stories, woven throughout this book, give readers a front-row seat to the triumphs, pitfalls, and unpredictability of the start-up world.

An Accessible – and Necessary – Guide

At its core, *Start-Ups DECLASSIFIED* carries an essential message: **be careful.** Andriole's advice is not about stifling ambition but about channeling it wisely. Not in the sense of avoiding risk—risk is the currency of entrepreneurship—but in recognizing the sheer complexity of achieving success. Timing, luck, and skill must align for a start-up to thrive. As Andriole reminds us, luck alone will not suffice, nor will brilliant ideas without execution.

With unflinching honesty, the book dismantles popular myths about entrepreneurship—those romanticized notions of overnight success—and replaces them with actionable insights grounded in reality.

This book isn't just another entry in the start-up literature canon. It's a wake-up call. Andriole's emphasis on pragmatism sets it apart, urging readers to approach entrepreneurship with eyes wide open. The questions he poses and the frameworks he offers push founders to deeply interrogate their ideas, teams, and strategies before diving into the turbulent waters of building a company.

Touring Andriole's Trenches

Steve's personal journey—his "lessons from the trenches"—offers invaluable insights for navigating this rapidly evolving landscape. At DARPA, he witnessed firsthand how visionary leadership and a culture of innovation can lead to breakthroughs like the internet and GPS. His time at Safeguard Scientifics during the dot.com boom underscores the volatility of start-ups, where irrational exuberance can lead to both meteoric rises and devastating crashes. Perhaps most poignant are his reflections about companies like ListenLogic, where the challenges of team dynamics, funding, and competition illustrate the breadth of financial and relational costs.

These experiences ground Andriole's advice in hard-earned wisdom. And the stories aren't just anecdotes; they're lessons. Steve's "repair, rent, or replace" framework for decision-making, his emphasis on understanding market dynamics, and his advocacy for objective self-assessment as examples. Similarly, his emphasis on having a "Plan B"— and even a "Plan C"— is particularly resonant in today's unpredictable market. Start-ups must be prepared for revenue streams to dry up, key customers to vanish, or technologies to become obsolete.

For start-up founders, employees, and investors, Steve's lessons are invaluable. He consistently highlights the unpredictability of success and the constant need for adaptability. And that no amount of planning can eliminate risk entirely—but understanding how to manage uncertainty is crucial.

Breaking Down *Start-Ups* DECLASSIFIED

One of the book's strengths lies in its structured breakdown of the startup lifecycle. Each chapter provides targeted insights that build upon one another, forming a comprehensive, accessible, and actionable blueprint for navigating the startup landscape. Some examples include:

- The chapter on *Innovation, Entrepreneurialism & Commercialization* delves into the foundational aspects of creating and scaling a startup. Andriole makes an important distinction between innovation and commercialization, emphasizing that having a great idea is not enough—execution is everything. This chapter helps founders understand how to move from ideation to sustainable business models, while also shedding light on the critical role of timing and market readiness.

- The chapter on *Technology Trends & Opportunities* is particularly relevant in today's fast-moving landscape. AI, automation, low-code platforms, and sustainability are all dissected with a keen eye for their long-term impact. Andriole does an excellent job of explaining not just what these trends are, but how they intersect with business models and investment decisions.

- His discussion of *Start-Up Skills & Competencies* is a must-read for any founder wondering what it takes to lead a startup successfully. From project management to persuasion skills, the list Andriole presents serves as a roadmap for personal and professional growth. What makes this discussion stand out is its emphasis on balance—technical prowess alone won't make you successful, nor will charisma without substance.

- The chapter on *Building & Growing Start-Ups* provides crucial insights into the mechanics of scaling a company. Andriole emphasizes the importance of assembling the right team, fine-tuning product-market fit, and understanding the nuances of funding and growth strategies. This chapter acts as a reality check for founders who believe that scaling is simply about increasing revenue—it's about building sustainable processes, fostering culture, and ensuring the startup is structurally prepared for expansion.

- The discussion about *Exiting Start-Ups* is another standout, describing the harsh reality of exits—whether through acquisition, IPO, or unfortunately, failure. Andriole doesn't just focus on the types of exits but also the psychology behind them. Understanding when to pivot, when to hold firm, and when to cut losses is a skill that can mean the difference between financial success and years of wasted effort.

The Special Role of AI

As Steve astutely observes, we are entering an era defined by artificial intelligence (AI). AI is no longer an emerging technology; it is a transformative force reshaping industries and redefining the rules of entrepreneurship. *Start-Ups DECLASSIFIED* provides timely guidance on how start-ups can harness the power of AI while piloting through its challenges. The academic use case illustrates how all this can happen faster than most believe it can.

As Steve repeats, AI has democratized access to capabilities that were once the domain of large enterprises. Tools like OpenAI's ChatGPT, Jasper, and Synthesia are enabling start-ups to automate tasks, create content, and optimize processes at unprecedented speeds and scales. This levels the playing field, allowing small teams to achieve what once required vast resources. For instance, companies like Synthesia are revolutionizing video content creation, while Jasper is transforming marketing workflows.

But the democratization of AI also brings new complexities. With foundational AI tools widely accessible, differentiation becomes a critical challenge. The market is saturated with AI-powered solutions, and start-ups must find unique ways to stand out. Success lies not just in leveraging AI but in integrating it with deep domain expertise to address specific, high-value problems and opportunities. Start-ups that fail to do so risk being lost in the noise.

In the next two to three years, start-ups will face a dual-edged sword of opportunity and complexity. AI will continue to lower barriers to entry, enabling more start-ups to launch innovative products. However, this accessibility will also lead to market saturation. Start-ups must embrace specialization, carving out niches where they can excel.

Ethical challenges around AI—including privacy, bias, and account-ability—will become more pronounced, prompting increased regulatory scrutiny. Start-ups that proactively address these issues will not only sur-vive but thrive. For instance, companies that specialize in AI for health-care, are already demonstrating the value of domain-specific solutions. Similarly, start-ups focused on sustainability—using AI to optimize energy consumption or supply chains—are poised for growth.

Steve argues throughout *Start-Ups DECLASSIFIED* that AI will impact start-up opportunities and challenges in ways we cannot even define today.

It is more critical than ever to monitor market trends and anticipate market shifts. Be sure to stay ahead of emerging trends and be prepared to pivot as needed. And importantly, build and cultivate resilience. Start-ups that diversify revenue streams and cultivate adaptable teams will be better able to weather economic volatility.

Prescriptions for the Future

What sets *Start-Ups DECLASSIFIED* apart is its unflinching honesty and actionable advice. Andriole's insights are not theoretical musings but grounded in real-world experience. The book is a treasure trove of lessons for anyone seeking to navigate the unpredictable waters of entrepreneur-ship. It's not just a guide; it's a compass for building, scaling, and sustain-ing start-ups in an age of rapid technological change.

As you delve into this book, let Steve Andriole's wisdom inspire and challenge you. Entrepreneurship is not a game of chance; it's a disci-pline that demands strategy, resilience, and unrelenting focus. *Start-Ups DECLASSIFIED* equips you with the tools and mindset to succeed in an era defined by AI, innovation, complexity, and constant change. The future belongs to those who are prepared—and this book is central to that preparation.

David G. Henkin

David Henkin is an expert in architecting and implementing innovative business strategies and solutions improving performance, profitable possibilities, and developing organizational capabilities through a collaborative-growth approach. His work experience includes Chief Innovation Officer at Vertex (VERX), where he also served as Executive Vice President. He launched and led Vertex's public cloud business as well as their managed services and outsourcing practice. David was a board member at Wheelhouse Analytics from startup through successful strategic acquisition. He also served as Chief Operating Officer at Coates Analytics from startup through successful strategic acquisition. Prior to that David was a Corporate Officer and Principal at Vanguard serving in their institutional and retail businesses, strategy and technology. David moved to Vanguard from Accenture where he managed large, complex programs in their communications industry group. The author of several books, he has taught in top-rated university business school programs while also serving as an innovator, consultant, and coach for corporate and nonprofit leaders in the areas of innovation, work design, business-technology, teams, and leadership among others.

Introduction

Here We Go

11 Questions and 21 Steps

You're an entrepreneur, right?

Then please explain why your entrepreneurial adventure makes sense by answering the following 11 questions as concisely and convincingly as possible:

1. What problem are you trying to solve?
2. Is it a big problem or a small one? How big is the market for your solution?
3. Has anyone else tried to solve the problem? How are they solving it? Have they been successful or unsuccessful? Why?
4. What's your unique solution to the problem? Is it technology-based? If so, what's so different about your technology solution? Do you have any current or pending intellectual property (IP)?
5. What are the barriers to entry? Can your solution be easily copied especially by large competitors? Or is it difficult to copy (beyond any IP)? How crowded is the space?
6. Is your *solution* a product or a service? Describe the unique features of the product or service: is it incremental or disruptive?
7. What are your founder strengths—and weaknesses? Why is your team solid? What is their product or service experience? Has it been successful or unsuccessful?
8. How much money do you need to execute? How much to launch, how much to an MVP, and how much to go to market?
9. Describe the projects and milestones necessary to launch.
10. What are the revenue projections? What are projected expenses? What are the risks?

11. What's the fundraising plan? How many fundraising relationships do you have? How persuasive is your pitch? Is it investor ready? Who are the pitch targets? What's the pitch schedule?

If you *can't* answer these questions, you're not an entrepreneur—and you're not an investor either. You have two choices: go back to the drawing board for the answers or—if that fails—get out of the game.

If you *can* answer the questions, take the following 21 steps:

1. Plot your path to personal wealth well before you launch. You should think about how to get rich—filthy rich—before you write one line of code or define the service you plan to offer. All of your investors do exactly the same thing every time they write a check. You're starting a business because you want to create generational wealth, not because you want to open free medical clinics in the third world. Does it matter that most startups fail? Hell, no. You should believe you're the exception, and that you will generate unimaginable piles of money in a few short years. If you die, you die. But you should not die without dreaming about a house in the Hamptons and a private jet. This is why you never sleep.

2. Think about who will buy your company or how to sell your company to shareholders through an initial public offering (IPO). You should think about this at the beginning of your journey, not along the way or at the end. Despite what the focus police tell you, you should think about exits every God damn day.

3. Find some IP you can monetize. It's essential to any differentiation argument you make. Without IP, there are no real barriers to entry (but know that IP is a far from perfect barrier).

4. Learn how to speak greed. It's a simple language that everyone can understand. It communicates only a few messages: how can I, we, and you get rich as quickly as possible, and how can we get started as quickly as possible?

5. Create products and services that sell into huge markets. Sure, there's money in legacy system upgrades and certain niche markets, but there's more in AI for everyone. The best business? Smart hardware or software to companies or—better—to the masses.

6. Build a team that's greedy, smart, and driven, and if it's not, rebuild it. If you're sentimental, you will fail. If there was ever a time to be a badass, this is it. Take no prisoners.

7. Respect the roles that luck, timing, personalities, relationships, and randomness play in the start-up process. You should assume a chaotic, unpredictable journey. If you're a planner, you're not an entrepreneur. If you can take a punch, you have a chance.

8. Don't waste time with people who cannot help you launch, build, and exit—or people everyone thinks are idiots or jerks. Because you will be judged by the professional friends you have, avoid Professor Bozo, Incompetent Charlie, and Mean Carol. Avoid close talkers, low talkers, and people who talk too much.

9. Make sure you're aware of what's happening around you—because there's always something happening around you. Death, illness, divorce, family, sex, drugs, and drinking, among other events that impact the success or failure of every startup. Deal with everything quickly and without remorse. Guilt is an anchor around your neck.

10. Tall, attractive people with the right hair, personal and professional connections, country clubs, and university pedigrees are essential to success, regardless of how many times you've heard about meritocracies—which, by the way, have never existed. Harvard and Stanford graduates are *better* than graduates from Kentucky and West Virginia State, though you should know—if you don't already—that degrees get you in the door but never guarantee success. The real value is the confidence they generate with investors who have never heard of Kentucky and West Virginia State but sure as hell have heard of Harvard and Stanford.

11. Remember that many Managing General Partners of large private equity venture funds know very little about technology. Play the game. Treat them like they're smart, even when your head feels like it's going to explode. But make damn sure that you and your team understand every nuance of emerging technology—and learn to tolerate the uninitiated.

12. *Pitching* is a huge, permanent part of your life. If you cannot pitch persuasively, you will not survive—which, by the way, is why so many startups die. Learn to pitch with the best or don't take the mound.

13. Remember that business models are temporary and revenue projections are hypotheses. Don't spend any time refining a business model template—like the *Business Model Canvas*—that will be obsolete the moment the market tells you what works and what doesn't. The only time you should engage in *canvassing* is when your investors insist. Then check all the boxes as sincerely as you can while assuring them that templates are always helpful, even though they're not.

14. The display of *passion* is necessary because investors have passion on their due diligence checklists, not because it predicts to success. They need to tell everyone at the Monday morning investment committee meeting that you're passionate, *really* passionate. So display it—as passionately as you can.

15. Don't ever take money from friends or family unless you're prepared for the relationships to die over money—which they will the minute your startup dies.

16. Never abdicate all legal and banking matters to your part-time Chief Financial Officer (CFO) or your part-time general counsel. You must educate yourself. If you rely completely upon CFOs and lawyers, you will suffer as they pleasure themselves with your ignorance.

17. Beware of *good guy* references. I cannot tell you how many times professionals who were described as really, really *good guys* turned out to be rude and incompetent. Do your own human due diligence.

18. Communicate frequently with your investors and Directors. Do not divide and conquer—a popular technique among naïve (or unethical) entrepreneurs. Provide whatever materials they request—especially financial records.

19. Outsource your Chief Marketing Officers (CMOs) and salespersons. Most of them bring experience that's irrelevant to your company. Start-up sales performance is almost always poor, so be prepared to pivot—a lot. One thing to remember: even though you're a startup, do not give away much equity to full-time sales and marketing professionals. Make them earn it. The confident ones will welcome performance-based equity. The bad ones will want as much equity as they can get before they sell anything.

20. Accept the equity distribution conundrum for what it is. While you want to incentivize key persons with equity, you also want to protect

as much as you can for yourself and future investors, regardless of how sure you are that climbing valuations will justify a growing cap table. Balance *good greed* with sound incentives management.

21. Look in the mirror every day. Are you cut out for this? Can you make tough decisions? Can you fire your friends? Can you tell white lies— and maybe some really black ones? Can you work on three hours sleep? Can you skip family outings? Can you travel at a moment's notice? Can you resist sex at the office? Can you do all this and a whole lot more? Look in the mirror before you start.

OK, you've answered the questions and taken the steps. Now it's time to read the book, which will inform, terrify, and test you. It says the quiet things out loud. But mostly the book is about increasing the probability of success. It leapfrogs the nonsense that permeates start-up myths, movies, and the limited series streaming on Netflix. The stories here alone are worth the price of admission.

Let's get started.

CHAPTER 1

Lessons From the Trenches

I've had a lot of innovation and entrepreneurial experiences in my career. Some good and some absolutely horrible. But overall it's been positive—and counting: even now, I have a few companies that might generate some nice returns, though I also have some investments that I'm sure will die heinous deaths.

But let's look at the journey that generated the lessons I've learned—lessons that might just help you navigate the same challenging waters I've navigated for decades. If the steps (and missteps) I've taken over the years can enable you to skip some of the more painful lessons, then I've accomplished what I set out to do—which is to accelerate your journey toward a successful start-up—and exit! Never forget that this journey is about money for all those who participate in the process. The ones who love to talk about how inspiring and rewarding the journey was are the ones who made money. Entrepreneurs who fail—which are the vast majority—seldom talk about how inspiring or rewarding the process was. I love how rich entrepreneurs do podcasts on lessons learned and spew *likes* on LinkedIn as the failures try to pay off their debts. No one wants to hear from losers. One-hit wonders are the best. As Mark Cuban likes to remind us, lots of success is explained by luck. Getting lucky—*once*—does not make you a serial entrepreneur. It just makes you lucky. All good, but don't bet on luck as your path to success. If you're a one-hit wonder, be sure to thank *luck* whenever you give a TED talk.

Let's set the stage for this historical journey. Yes, it's to demonstrate some credibility, but it's also to describe some lessons that might really help you stay sober about the start-up process.

The Defense Advanced Research Projects Agency (DARPA)

I started my innovation and entrepreneurial career at DARPA—the Defense Advanced Research Projects Agency—in the 1970s. DARPA is an amazing place that since 1958 has always funded very smart people who fund the research of even smarter ones. I worked with Bob Kahn and Vint Cerf—the co-fathers of the internet—and George Heilmeier and Craig Fields, both DARPA Directors with similar management styles and brilliant minds.

Way back then—the 1970s—we all had email (courtesy of the ARPANET).

We had checkbooks.
We had staff cars.
We had helicopters.
We had planes—and when we flew to Europe, we flew on the Concord.

We ran what was essentially a public equity venture fund funded annually with taxpayer—*other peoples'*—money. In fact, DARPA is not all that different from conventional private equity venture capital (VC) funds that raise money from public pension funds, endowments, corporations, and high-net-worth individuals. Of course, there is one major difference: at DARPA, we did it for intellectual excitement, career advancement, and bragging rights, not to get filthy rich, the private equity venture capitalist's raison d'être—though we absolutely did love the power and fame (every time we boarded a DOD helicopter, spent some time on a Navy aircraft carrier, or flew on the Concord). Compared with my corporate friends—the ones I funded—I made hardly any money at DARPA. No one did.

DARPA was the most amazing experience of my career. Perhaps sadly, this, by definition, means that everything that came after DARPA was unsatisfying. This is not entirely true, because there were highs after DARPA, but it's easily safe to say that if you ever have an opportunity to work at a place like DARPA, grab it without hesitation (noting, of course, there are really no places like DARPA). It's also safe to say that I learned more about innovation and entrepreneurialism during that time than I did in any of my subsequent times in industry and academia combined.

For those unfamiliar with DARPA, here's a short list of its accomplishments (McCallion, 2020):

- The Internet
- Windows
- World Wide Web
- Videoconferencing
- Google Maps
- GPS
- Siri
- Unix (and the Cloud)
- Urban Photonic Sandtable Display
- Internet Anonymity/Onion Routing
- BigDog (Boston Dynamics Atlas Robot)
- Cyborg Insects
- Graphical User Interface (GUI) and the Mouse
- Virtual Reality
- Drones
- Digital Libraries
- High Energy Lasers
- Stealth Vehicles
- Autonomous Ships
- Universal Translator
- Brain-Neural Interface Chips and Brain-Interfacing Machines, and so on

As my career evolved, I reflected more and more on the DARPA culture and its approach to innovation, entrepreneurialism, and commercialization. I also compared it with corporate innovation and entrepreneurialism, which, for so many reasons, is grossly unfair to corporate innovation and entrepreneurialism. I wrote about this in detail in *Forbes Magazine* (Andriole, 2015).

Probably the most innovative team we funded from the Cybernetics Technology Office (CTO) was Nick Negroponte's Architecture Machine Group at MIT. This group evolved into MIT's Media Lab. We also funded some pioneers in artificial intelligence and natural language processing and some—like myself (Andriole, 1976)—who created technologies and systems that monitored and predicted global events.

Here are some takeaways from these early experiences that apply to any entrepreneurial activity you might pursue:

- There's a definite "entrepreneurial establishment" in the United States and throughout the world—the entrepreneurial power centers that drive a huge percentage of entrepreneurial activity. Stanford University is more powerful than Penn State, just as Google, Nvidia, and OpenAI are more powerful than Deloitte, PWC, or KPMG. Innovators and entrepreneurs have hierarchies and *royalty* like every other activity in the world. If you cannot be knighted yourself, befriend some Jedi Knights. But make sure you don't swim upstream trying, for example, to convince the world that there's entrepreneurial activity at Penn State that rivals the entrepreneurial spirit at Stanford, MIT, or Carnegie-Mellon. That's a suicide mission that might make you popular at Penn State but will not get you into entrepreneurial heaven.

- If you don't have immediate access to the national or global entrepreneurial establishment, you can exploit local and regional entrepreneurial establishments to your advantage. But remember that the scale of your endeavors (and rewards) will be as large or small as the size of the local, regional, national, or global establishment you join. In other words, the innovation and entrepreneurial game is different depending on the playing field.

- Regardless of where you play the game, you should adjust your expectations accordingly and network, network, and network some more: you can never know too many people.

- Yes, it helps when the ideas are indisputably brilliant, but brilliance is contextual: it must be surrounded by the right pedigrees, repertoires, and Jedi Knights. Brilliance without context isn't brilliant—or even important. It's the guy who really invented electric cars (not Elon Musk), the light bulb (not Thomas Edison), and the telephone (not Alexander Graham Bell). Trust me, there are lots more who never got any credit for their brilliance. But look who received the notoriety and made the money. As we'll discuss later, there's a world of difference among innovation, entrepreneurialism, and commercialization.

International Information Systems

When I left DARPA, I founded a company that focused on the design and development of software systems primarily for the U.S. Department of Defense and the U.S. Intelligence Community. It's what you did after DARPA if you didn't stay in the government, go to industry (usually to a company you funded while at DARPA), or land in academia. It was 1980. We developed a prototyping methodology—*storyboarding*—that enabled our clients to "see" before they developed expensive software applications (what we call *mockups* today). We did cognitive systems engineering for human–computer interaction (HCI). We developed interactive systems for the defense and intelligence communities. We built databases. The timing of the business model was good. It aligned with the requirements of our clients, who were all investing in interactive computer-based systems of one kind or another. I never thought of myself as an *entrepreneur* back then. It was before all the rage about start-ups and venture capitalists and how the world would never be the same when VCs and entrepreneurs started to date, marry, and have kids. I incorporated in Delaware. I did my own taxes. I worked out of my basement. I was an entrepreneur.

Is there a trick to starting a company? Sure, revenue. Anyone who's ever watched *Shark Tank* knows how many times Kevin O'Leary asks, "*do you have any sales?*" IIS started well—*very well*. Lots of contracts until the contacts dried up, people moved on, and programs ended. I then branched out to other sources of funds, including especially the Small Business Innovation Research (SBIR) program—which saved the company.

Lesson?

- Assume your first and best customers will die—and leave you out of the will. Make sure you have a solid Plan B (and a good Plan C).

The SBIR program funds lots of companies to do some innovative things—for excellent money—and the Phase II and Phase III contracts can make you rich by commercializing what the government pays you to create. Realizing this, I engaged some partners to write proposals that I submitted through my company. I was able to have it both ways. If the contract was awarded, I paid the partner, but if it wasn't, I didn't have to pay them a salary. They were contract employees to my company. No long-term salary burden, and I didn't have to do all the work. Think about this model. It works. The exact same strategy can work today. Use freelancers. Keep overhead low. Hire only full-time employees when you need to. *Keep your equity.*

Lesson?

- Think about SBIR and similar programs—especially before you go to friends, family, or venture capitalists for money. When your revenue stream is strong and you still need some cash, VCs will (mostly) come to you or at least *like* you when they hear your numbers. *Remember that SBIR funding is equity free—you get the money, and keep all of the equity in your company.*

Government contracts from government agencies, while great, come and go. If you place all your eggs in that—or any—basket, you may be fine, but you might also get caught in some change-of-leadership events, some program funding cycles, and some agency budget cuts—all unpredictable but inevitable events. The SBIR program has been around for decades and is still going strong, regardless of who's the president of the United States or which political party is in power.

George Mason University

I sold—*exited*—International Information Systems in 1985 and *retired* to George Mason University (GMU) where, under the leadership of the amazing (and still very much missed) Andy Sage, founded a new academic department, while Andy was founding an entire School of Information Technology and Engineering, now the Volgenau School of Engineering. I was the Chairman of the Department of Information Systems and Systems Engineering where we founded research centers that focused on command and control (Harry Van Trees), software systems engineering (Dick Fairley and Al Davis), and computer security (Sushil Jajodia). I also proudly held the George Mason Institute Endowed Professorship at GMU. I was very happy at GMU. I created new programs and courses and continued consulting for a variety of defense agencies. I liked the leadership there, and the leadership liked me. But for (good) personal reasons, I moved back to the Philadelphia area where I began a professional pivot from defense to corporate problem-solving which wasn't the best professional decision I've made in my career. In fact, aside from personal reasons, it was the worst career decision I ever made. I left my DARPA/DOD identity behind, which I could have monetized forever.

Lesson?

- Before you make a personal decision that dramatically impacts your professional life, think it through. Think about it very, very carefully—especially if it requires a professional pivot, which is tantamount to leaving your swim lane—maybe forever.

Drexel University

In 1990, I moved to Drexel University, where I founded the Center for Multidisciplinary Information Systems Engineering and served as a Professor of Information Systems and Electrical and Computer Engineering. The significant innovation during that time was the creation of the nation's first online Master's Program in Information Systems (MSIS) that was funded by the Alfred P. Sloan Foundation

(Andriole, 1997). I was fortunate again to work with gold in Frank Mayadas and Ralph Gomery and platinum in the Sloan Foundation.

Frank and Ralph created the field of asynchronous learning networks (ALNs), now simply known as online education. I was extremely fortunate to be part of that historic entrepreneurial journey (Mayadas, 1997). Maybe I should repeat that: in the 1990s, Sloan created online learning, which is now perhaps the primary way Americans learn.

Lessons?

- *Again*: Context explains as much of the variance in the innovation equation as anything else. Play with professionals— not amateurs—and learn to *objectively* (and quickly) distinguish between the two.
- Mistake? *I took my eye off the ball.* There were opportunities to commercialize asynchronous learning—*distance learning*—that I failed to pursue, so keep your eyes on the prize. *Let me say that again: I made a huge mistake.* I could have commercialized the innovation we created. *Keep your commercialization radar on all the time.*

Drexel appealed to Frank and Ralph because of its technological roots and because the Dean of the College of Information Studies at the time —Dick Lytle (also sorely missed)—never wavered from the moment the idea for an online master's program hit his ears. I had nothing to do with either of those events or the judgment exhibited by these professionals. It's who they already were. Frank also liked my DARPA experience—confirmation of the context-is-validation hypothesis (and the value of Jedi Knights).

The online Master's Program was above all else a *product* that had to work all of the time. It needed 24/7 support. It required upgrades. This was new to me. I learned a lot about what it takes to design, develop, and field a consumer product. Watch this process closely. It's different from R&D where the principal objective is the creation of intellectual capital that can be converted to intellectual property (IP) that can be monetized. You will need people who have done this before to succeed. Find them before you tell the world about your amazing product.

Lessons?

- *Go with your strength.* Stay the course that's worked for you and your team. I was able to exploit my DARPA identity and my DARPA network for a long time after I left the agency, though for good personal reasons, I pivoted to the corporate world, but in the process, set myself back as I built a new network comprised of more corporate than government technology professionals. It took me five years to build a reasonable corporate network among professionals who had never heard of DARPA. *Can you imagine?* In the Washington, DC area, DARPA is the shining city on the hill, but in the Philadelphia area, DARPA is a town no one knows exists. Remember that personal brand reinvention is even harder than company brand reinvention.

- The online program we developed at Drexel had all kinds of commercialization potential, including infrastructure, applications, services, and support. The technology was extensible to training in many different areas. Partnerships with emerging educational and training platforms were possible. Relationships with content providers could have been built. You get the idea. *Think as widely as possible beyond the immediate application.*

Cigna

From Drexel, I migrated to Cigna as Senior Vice President for Technology Strategy and its first CTO. Technology at Cigna was a brutally managed cost center with one goal in mind: reduce technology (and other) expenses to increase profitability. The company once actually suggested that email be shut down because it sapped productivity. (No, we never shut down email, but you get the point).

Lesson?

- While Cigna was technology-deprived in many ways back then, its motives were clear.[*] Those who made technology investment decisions were absolutely transparent, which was actually helpful. Leadership believed that technology sucked too much money out of operations—and they let everyone know it. If you're selling innovative products or services, make sure there are customers for your brilliance. Back then, Cigna did not care about technical brilliance. Technology was just about keeping the trains running on time, not finding new places to visit. Selling technology to technology adoption laggards can create a steady revenue stream, but it's not where entrepreneurs should spend much time. Never forget that context is critical to your innovation and entrepreneurial activities.

Lessons?

- Definitions of innovation and entrepreneurialism differ across companies and industries. Some—like entertainment and consumer electronics—embrace technological change. But some industries worry about how much technology spending will cut into profits—not how technology might reinvent their products and services—and then lead to profits.
- Start-ups targeted at high-margin industries are much better positioned than those targeted at low-margin industries. Here's a list of the highest-margin industries from IBIS (2024):

1. Trusts & Estates in the United States (60.9%)
2. Stock & Commodity Exchanges in the United States (51.5%)

---

[*] Cigna has smartly recently invested in AI to determine a customer's payment eligibility, improve patient outcomes, recommend roles to employees, make preliminary diagnoses, and help it process claims (Moran, 2023), which is a far cry from when I was there and new technology was mostly—shall we say—"unwelcome." Unfortunately, Cigna is now fighting some lawsuits that believe the company allegedly *"illegally used an artificial intelligence (AI) algorithm to deny hundreds of thousands of claims without a physician's review"* (Bendix, 2023).

3. Commercial Leasing in the United States (51.1%)
4. Private Equity, Hedge Funds & Investment Vehicles in the United States (48.9%)
5. Cigarette & Tobacco Manufacturing in the United States (47.8%)
6. Land Leasing in the United S (47.4%)
7. Snowplowing Services in the United States (42.0%)
8. Credit Card Issuing in the United States (41.5%)
9. Credit Bureaus & Rating Agencies in the United States (36.8%)
10. Venture Capital & Principal Trading in the United States (34.8%)

- High-margin targeting is often consistent with the search for *sloppy* revenue streams.

Sidebar

I just have to compare a DARPA experience with one I had at Cigna.

Shortly after I joined Cigna as its first CTO, I met with Bill Taylor—the Cigna CEO—to discuss some ideas I had regarding the technology infrastructure (which I believed needed some help). After some very pleasant introductions and a moment of chit-chat, I slipped Bill a sheet of paper with 10 items focused on technology investments designed to improve the technology infrastructure and improve the application development process. He looked at the page for about 5 seconds, spun it around, and pushed it back to me. He then told me to come back when there were only three things on the list, a request I understood. He ended the meeting by standing up and shaking my hand cordially. I think the entire meeting lasted about 10 minutes if it lasted that long. I never met with Bill again.

Some years earlier, I was invited to discuss a technology program at DARPA with George Heilmeier. I will never forget that the inventor of liquid crystal displays, a White House Fellow, the DARPA director, and a member of the National Inventors Hall of Fame—a true engineering legend—gave me 3 hours of his time—not just once, but several times.

Yes, I—and so should you—realize that Bill and George were from two different worlds. One sold insurance, and the other sold engineering. It's important to appreciate how fundamentally different executives see "technology" (Andriole, 2023). That's the takeaway. You must understand how different these perspectives—and markets—can be, and adjust your start-up plans accordingly. Among other talents, this is called *reading the room*—and by implication, *reading the market*.[†]

Safeguard Scientifics and TL Ventures

I left Cigna for greener pastures. I joined Safeguard Scientifics and TL Ventures as a Senior Vice President and CTO and venture fund Principal, respectively. I was hired to point Safeguard in the right technology investment direction and help TL Ventures conduct technology due diligence around their deals and warm some of the out-of-town board seats TL purchased as part of their investments. At Safeguard Scientifics and TL Ventures, we invested in many technology companies, and I experienced the start-up process from the perspective of a venture capitalist and operating investor rather than an innovator or entrepreneur—the flip side of the coin—though with very different modus operandi. We invested in too many companies in a very short period of time: it was the dot.com bubble, so why not? We took more than a few of those companies public, and one or two of them exist today in one form or another, sort of, maybe, but not really. Actually, they all died, were acquired or reborn with some amazing jujitsu. The best example of this was the Internet Capital Group (ICG), which was once worth $50B!

All in, the Safeguard family invested in over 100 companies in a few short years—at least that's what marketing told us. The entire Safeguard and TL Ventures orbit was home to so many companies that it was not unusual for me to walk into a meeting about one of our companies I never knew existed. Strange, I know, but I wasn't the only one asking *"who are these guys?"*

[†] Make sure you profile everyone in your professional orbit. George loved technology. Bill? Not so much. All good, though a few years after Bill retired and I left the company, there were technology problems at Cigna that cost shareholders tons of money, problems that were described as *self-inflicted wounds* (Bass, 2003). Timing is everything, isn't it?

A mea culpa: obviously not all these companies should have filed initial public offerings (IPOs). They were IPOed simply because they *could* be IPOed. Of course—and for the record—we sort of believed they had a chance to make it on the outside, but we also drank a lot of Kool-Aid. We exploited momentum as much as we could, which is what everyone does. The money was amazing—until it wasn't.

Lessons?

- IPO buyers beware (unless you're an insider).
- Be wary of investment climates described as "irrational exuber-ance," but understand how they can be exploited—and exploit them when you're sober—or *in the room* with well-informed stakeholders. *But exploit them, like what's happening with AI.* Understand?

The real fun at Safeguard was buying, selling, and investing in many different companies, and working closely with entrepreneurs and their technology teams. Some of these entrepreneurs were extraordinarily talented, but many were not: there was no shortage of incompe-tence.com back then. Everyone wanted to play in the bubble, even if they couldn't spell dot.com, though way too many could spell dot.con.

I was hired into a dual role: half of my time would be spent at Safeguard and half at TL Ventures. While I know that dual reporting relationships almost always fail, TL Ventures saved me by sending me to Safeguard full-time! I was beyond relieved—and excited. My office was moved right next to Pete Musser's, the charismatic and legendary founder of Safeguard (Warner, 2001), who—incredibly—was the inspiration for companies like Comcast/Xfinity, QVC, and Novell. Pete and I became fast friends and champions of Safeguard's Internet Infrastructure Investment Strategy, which we developed together.[‡] I'll never forget the day we sold $100,000,000 of stock to Textron after a meeting with Louis Campbell, Textron's CEO. I made our internet pitch, and Louis and Pete worked out the deal terms. I'll also never

---

[‡] While Pete was not a *technologist*, his instincts around how technology should be packaged for sale were superb.

forget a trip back from New York when Pete was struggling financially, and I suggested he sell some—not that much—stock from the companies in the Safeguard family to relieve some of the pressure—and when he told me he could never do that to the companies—*to his companies*. I'm still amazed how loyal Pete was to the companies in the Safeguard family even if it meant more financial pain for himself.

Lessons?

- Most of the Safeguard and TL Ventures companies were innovation incrementalists, not real disruptors, though nearly all of them—like all of the dot.coms—were sold to investors as disruptive. Investors were sold disruption everywhere, but most (not all) of the companies were just piggy-backing on business models and processes defined by others (and still very much in the prototyping phase). Claims of disruption grew every year, even among companies whose business models never really changed. Such was the time: if *internet* wasn't in every slide of every pitch deck, you were somehow *old*, and no one would give you money.

- But if you were an *internet company*, then, well, insane valuations were easy. *Just the way it is today with all things AI.* Pay close attention to where the money's flowing, and process the trajectories carefully. If they make sense and have some legs, they make sense, but if they're irrationally exuberant, then you better be pretty good at timing, while you control your greed genes.

- Control the messaging around your company with customers, vendors, and suppliers. Don't worry too much about how quants and spreadsheet jockeys describe your start-up. Keep descriptions about your business model, products, services, team, and use cases *simple and consistent*: own your brand all the way down to the tweet. Resist temptations to overhype your company's capabilities even when you're in the middle of some irrational market exuberance—but don't resist completely. Understand?

- If you're an investor, check out the real company, not the one on a website. Find some consultants with no vested interest in the company you're assessing. You need them because entrepreneurs and existing investors know how to paint gorgeous murals that fade over time. Try as best you can to control the emotions around the process. Everyone falls in love with companies, markets, CEOs, and technologies. But love often turns to anger when they realize they just wrote a huge check after a night of bad due diligence. That said, irrational exuberance can be exploited. It's all about timing.

The rise and fall of Safeguard Scientifics tracks perfectly with the rise and fall of the dot.coms. Lots of companies, investors, and venture funds played in the bubble until it burst. The point is simple: investors often succeed because of what other people—and markets—do. Most—though not all—of the internet wonders just followed someone else's ideas until they crashed and burned. Once that happened, investors also crashed and burned (Primack, 2014). In this case, the Internal Rates of Return (IRRs) across many private equity VC funds, and the stock price of companies like Safeguard, tracked with the rise and fall of the dot.coms.

Once the bubble burst—even though there was still tons of money to be made in digital technology—many venture funds and companies (see Figure 1.1) imploded. The Safeguard ending is especially sad, because few companies had ever risen to the heights Safeguard reached in the late 1990s.

I don't think there's any better way to discuss the rise and fall of Safeguard (SFE) than its stock price over time. Before and after the bubble burst, the stock was flat, despite changes in leadership and board members, and historically positive market conditions for technology companies (especially after 2009). It exploited the bubble but missed opportunities to invest in way underpriced technology companies from 2001 to 2003, to participate in a recovering market from 2003 to 2009, and then a technology rally since then. I believe Safeguard under-leveraged the investment credibility it earned while in the bubble (Key, 2001), and completely missed the technology market that loved the

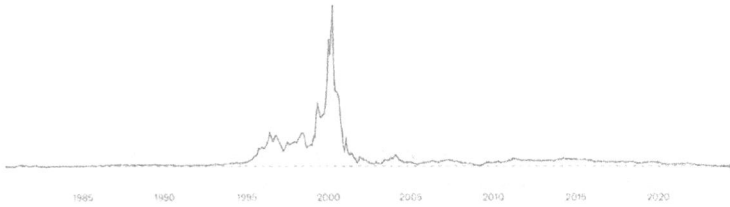

Figure 1.1 Safeguard's stock history

Source: The NY Stock Exchange.

cloud, software-as-a-service (SaaS), analytics, blockchain, and cryptocurrency (among other technologies)—not to mention today's exuberance around AI. Who knows how many start-ups and early-stage companies Safeguard could have worked to the advantage of its shareholders. While I understand that the circumstances in 2001 were, shall we say, "challenging," I also believe that a creative pivot was possible.

In fairness, there were lots of postbubble losers, because there are always mimics and copycats. These investors were looking to exploit what looked like easy opportunities to make money. They're momentum players. They eat what others kill.

Safeguard became a "lifestyle" public company. Pete Musser felt the same way. In at least 10 conversations I had with him over the years after he left Safeguard (over ham and cheese sandwiches with Higgins resting at his side), he felt Safeguard was just standing still for reasons he could not fully understand (though he was always careful never to directly criticize the company he founded). In his infectious, affable way, he listed some investment opportunities he felt could be hit out of the park and hoped Safeguard would see them the same way. By the way, in 2024 Safeguard Scientifics filed Form 25 to Voluntarily Delist its Common Stock from The Nasdaq Stock Market.

Lessons?

- A lifestyle business is not *the* "exit" that you want unless there are no other exit opportunities. But is that all bad? There are many rich entrepreneurs who settled into lifestyle businesses that paid them incredibly well to just stand still. Think about it when you fail to execute a splashy exit for your start-up (much more on this later).

- Watch for market signals. Today, entrepreneurs can sell anything *AI*. But will that exuberance continue forever? Nothing lasts forever regardless of how important a technology might be. Safeguard was one of the most successful companies in the country during the dot.com days. When dot.coms lost their luster, Safeguard was caught flatfooted. No Plan B. No Plan C. As already suggested, everyone needs a plan when the wheels come off—*because they will come off*—which is why selling a company at the right time usually makes sense (just ask Mark Cuban about timing).

Deals Along the Way

After Safeguard and TL Ventures, I founded and cofounded three additional companies. One focused on business technology services—the Acentio Group—and one—Ascendigm, LLC—unsuccessfully attempted to build a consortium of professionals around the government's SBIR program—the same program that saved my first company. One of the consulting companies exists today and provides professional services to corporate clients, but it's just a tiny company. Ascendigm and Acentio are long gone (though I still have some golf towels with the company names on them). TechVestCo—the strategic technology consulting company—is still around and has served some important clients very well.

I was part of some other companies as well. ePrivacy Group spun off a company—Turntide—that was sold to Symantec. That transaction was fortuitous. David Brussin developed some unique antispam router technology that was sold to Symantec. David and Vince Schiavone, Stephen Cobb, James Koenig, and Michael Miora cofounded the ePrivacy Group, but at Turntide, the ePrivacy spinoff, David saved the day.

Then there was ListenLogic, where I was a major investor. ListenLogic was a really interesting and timely unstructured social data analytics company, that was finally sold to Anexinet in 2016 after eight long years marked by the coming and going of multiple CFOs, CMOs, analysts, salespersons, presidents, CEOs, and board members. The technology part of the holding company (UDA, LLC)—Akuda Labs—ended with an "acqui-hire" by Target. Lots of Angel investors left the table poorer and angry.

Sadly, very sadly, many of the Angel investors in ListenLogic never made another Angel investment in their lives. Yes, a lot of people lost a lot of money—including me—but let's face it, Angel investors should assume some risk, some level of unpredictability—and worse. Again, timing is also often everything. Had ListenLogic pursued a soft, tease of an offer from a consulting company, everyone might have left the table exchanging self-congratulatory high-fives; years later, investors left the table disappointed and angry—especially when they heard that Radian6 —which was also a social media monitoring company—was acquired by Salesforce for $326M.

Lessons?

- Vet, vet, and vet some more—and be wary of entrepreneurs unable to self-fund or use their professional networks to raise enough money to support *strategies* that make sense. *Make sure you vet ideas with smart people who have nothing to do with your company.*

- If you're an investor, *make sure the operating agreements provide investors with adequate access to information about how the company is governed and how the money is spent* (much more on this later).

- If you're an entrepreneur, *make sure you surround yourself with professionals who will tell you the truth*—and make sure they— *and you*—have open minds about what's smart and workable. Balance your need for control with the desire to succeed. No one can start, build, and exit a company alone. Remain aware of your personal alienation score. If it's high, reach out for help before there's no one left to help you succeed.

- *Watch revolving doors that spin a lot*: if a company rotates professionals in and out on a regular basis, there's a larger problem. An indisputable early warning indicator of probable failure is a spinning door. Listen to the people who leave and try to fix why they left (or were *fired*).

- *Entrepreneurs must keep all eyes on the competitive ball.* Technology changes so fast that it's essential to remain vigilant about competition. This is not a drive-by activity; it's a continuous, dedicated task. Entrepreneurs should be prepared to discuss all competitors in detail whenever an investor or customer asks.

- *Watch your relationships.* As a long-term champion of ListenLogic, when the company was finally sold and Angel investors were disappointed by the return on their investments, part of my reputation crashed and burned. I never heard from several of the investors I convinced to write checks again. Some personal relationships were destroyed. So be careful. (I covered some of the losses, but not enough.)

I even invested in a restaurant—Avero in Wayne, Pennsylvania—which is an embarrassing mistake because I pride myself on being at least a semi-disciplined investor in technology companies, not "craft pizza." But sometimes we do things for reasons other than money. I was a dumb Angel who lost all his pizza money. Everyone did (I think). So stay in your lane.

I earned a small piece of a technology services company—LiquidHub—as a long-term member of the founding Board of Directors. Shares were granted for my board service, and I cashed three really nice checks along an 18-year journey. The good news is that the principal investor—Chrys Capital—bought enough revenue (through acquisitions) to earn a 2× offer from Capgemini who bought the company in 2018. Everyone was happy. Thanks, guys, for getting this done: LiquidHub is actually a textbook example of how to create and grow a start-up and then exit a successful mid-sized company.

If a company has been around for years but reports only modest, barely profitable growth, it's likely to fail. ListenLogic entered a white-hot market—social media analytics—at the right time. Lots of competitors were in the space. But many of these companies were better funded by institutional VCs (or deep pocket companies) with the right connections (Lasica and Bale, 2011), not Angels who had little or no understanding of what social media analytics is. Because they were better funded, the competitors could capture larger market shares and polish their value propositions. The company struggled with messaging, marketing, sales, and product development almost from the beginning. Worse, the company worried way too much about funding. When I studied Pitchbook's analysis of the field and the players, ListenLogic had 24 competitors that, in many cases, were venture-backed. Inside Social Media (Lasica and Bale, 2011) identified 20+ social media listening companies. I was surprised to see that ListenLogic was not on the list of the top 40, though, fortunately, was listed as one of the *other* (30+) monitoring services.

Lessons?

- Do not attempt to alter human nature during your innovation/entrepreneurial journey. It is what it is, and always will be. When you encounter over-the-top irrationality, walk away. If there's irrationality on your team, eliminate it, and if it's among your investors, marginalize it—if you discovered the irrationality too late. (If you discovered it before the investment, shame on you for taking the money.)
- If you're an investor in an irrational enterprise, try to influence leadership. If that doesn't work, then work with the other investors to affect change. Ultimately, if the change is beyond reach, then stop investing and become an activist investor to unseat the irrational entrepreneurs and leadership teams. None of this is pretty, pleasant, or easy, which is why God made *due diligence* and why concepts like "buyer beware" have so much staying power.
- As is still and always the case, people with the right hair, personal and professional connections, country clubs, and university pedigrees can easily get their hands on money. Many manag-

ing general partners of large private equity venture funds often know very little about digital technology, yet manage hundreds of millions of pension fund (and other) dollars to invest in technology start-ups and early-stage companies. There's a reason why this all works, and it has nothing to do with hard work. Just accept all this as one of world's start-up mysteries. (Actually, it's no mystery at all.)

- Let's operationalize this: how many members of your team have Ivy League degrees, have *standing* in the business community, are members of entrepreneurial power centers, play golf at the clubs where your investors play, and know the same *good guys*? None? Find some.

- How many relationships does your team have with venture capitalists and professional Angel investors who have funded successful companies? How many *warm introductions* can you make, arrange, or receive? None? Find some.

- Remember that there's perhaps no greater clubby club than VC. Find a way into the club; find ways into all of the clubs, or at least as many as you can.

- Entrepreneurs: note the *relative devaluation* of *subject matter expertise* in the investment community. Remember investment success is often not entirely about subject matter expertise. You will therefore have to sometimes inform and educate what your company plans to do and why it could make everyone rich and famous (for getting rich). These lectures must be skillfully delivered to students who often believe they're already well-educated and informed, that is, believe they're smarter than they actually are (a normal human condition). But at the end of the day, no matter how good a professor you are, or how brilliant your ideas may be, Angels and private equity venture capitalists have the checkbooks. Deal with them respectfully if you want their money. Learn how to communicate with them in short phrases and sound bites, and *never* challenge their ignorance, no matter how obvious, easy, appealing, or entertaining it might be.

- *Also note the importance of fundraising relationships here and note it well.* How a venture fund raises money is the venture firm's business, not yours, but be sure to research where the money comes from, how much the firm has raised, and what the general investment strategy is. Make sure you also profile the managing partners, and never forget that all investors are heat-seeking missiles searching for personal wealth by leveraging their personal and professional relationships—and that's all they really are—*not that there's anything wrong with that!*
- *At the end of the day, relationships rule.*

Shire Pharmaceuticals

In 2010, I joined Shire Pharmaceuticals as the Interim Chief Information Officer (CIO). This was an interesting assignment for sure. Shire's technology infrastructure needed some investment as did its technology governance. Here was my initial agenda:

- Reorganize for improved effectiveness and accountability
- Re-define the IT operating model
- Control and measure processes, especially spend
- Fill critical skills gaps
- Communicate with the company about plans, progress, and capabilities

The list of projects I launched included:

- Re-organization
- Video teleconferencing
- Wireless security
- Business resumption planning and disaster recovery
- Business process mapping/management
- Emerging technology-driven R&D
- Infrastructure refresh
- Audit compliance
- Aggregate spend reporting

- Global CRM
- Rapid global provisioning
- Client support (end-user, helpdesk, and VIP)
- Enterprise/global (information/applications) architecture
- Performance assessment/management
- Sourcing

All good, but I could not help but notice that there were a lot of people whose jobs were, shall we say, unclear. I noticed that lots of employees were effectively "tenured." It appeared to me that they didn't actually work that hard—and that no one really expected them to: the office was quiet after 5; dead after 6. They were unsupervised. Lots of politics. Lots of passive aggression. It was like Cigna in so many ways—*and the perfect opposite of the work culture entrepreneurs must create.*

I noticed that underperforming vendors underperformed with impunity—until we replaced them (incredibly, often much to their surprise). Everyone seemed distracted, including the Board of Directors to which I presented several times.

In retrospect, it felt like the company was constantly dressing up for an acquisition, which finally occurred in 2019 *for a ton of money—$62B* —which was *one of the largest deals in pharma history* (Parrish, 2024).

So how could all this be true? Revenue: Shire owned the drug Adderall and its descendants.

When it's raining cash, you can afford to be a little, shall we say, *sloppy*. My requests for additional budget were never refused.

Like Cigna, Shire was a cash machine. But unlike Cigna, at least when I was there, Shire was willing to invest in technology.

Lesson?

- *Massive revenue streams enable companies to be administratively, operationally, organizationally, managerially, and strategically sloppy.* Savvy entrepreneurs—like savvy management consultants—know where to find sloppy. *Look for it.* As noted, some industries have higher profit margins than others. Sloppy lives in these industries, not the low-margin ones. Follow the money.

Villanova University

My time at Villanova has been wonderfully "complicated." I joined the faculty as the Thomas G. Labrecque Professor of Business Technology in 2001—*thank you again to the Labrecque family*—full of new ideas about curriculum, delivery, research, and funding.[§] I prepared a 75-page slide deck on possible new revenue streams. I suggested new majors and minors. I identified lots of opportunities for executive education. I identified sponsored research opportunities—including SBIRs. I even wrote three columns in *Forbes Magazine* as a back door into the university's MBA strategy. At nearly every turn, except one—I finally got an undergraduate minor and an MBA Specialization in AI going[¶]—I was told in one way or another that leadership had little or no interest in my ideas (but didn't have the heart to tell me so out loud).

That aside, there's good reason why Villanova is a place where new ideas are often tabled. The university has experienced record-high undergraduate applications: not surprisingly, everyone wants to go to Villanova! But suffice it to say that Villanova is not a crazy trailblazer—and why should it be? It's a near-perfect example of a "*if it ain't broke, don't fix it*" business model. My ideas should have never been developed or shared. It took me way too long to fully appreciate my entrepreneurial irrelevance!

Villanova is an unequaled undergraduate success story—a master class in how to deliver quality undergraduate education. But as nice as everyone can mostly be, it's not somewhere an entrepreneur—an aggressive change agent—will feel comfortable. Change—*especially disruptive change*—is just not part of the culture—and, let's face it, probably shouldn't be. When something's working well, let it work, but, and as I've suggested several times, there should always be a backup plan. The good times never roll on forever. Pandemics and economic crashes happen. All organizations should plan for the worst.

[§] I live in the Villanova School of Business at Villanova University.
[¶] It took me almost three years to convince everyone that AI courses would benefit our students. But I prevailed!

Lessons?

- I did not read the room before I accepted the position at Villanova. I was recruited to believe that I'd be able to innovate across the board. I should have validated the recruitment pitch. I should have studied the culture and players more closely. *Learn how to read the room and everyone in it!*

- You must make realistic assessments of what's possible and—if you're developing your own start-up culture—what's desirable. This is true for you, your investors, your teams, and your customers.

- *Your ability to separate promotion from authenticity is existential.* Many professionals talk a good game, but when push comes to shove, they're nowhere to be found. The promoters who recruited me into Villanova were not, shall we say, entirely authentic. They knew my ideas would probably be dead on arrival but told me that I was exactly what they needed to breathe new life into the place! I was excited. But as it turned out, I was the one who needed the defibrillator! This promoter-versus-authentic distinction skill is especially important when you're recruiting your team, when you're raising money, as you develop your corporate culture and as you evolve your business model.

- Plan B (and Plan C) is every start-up's requirement.

TechVestCo

TechVestCo, LLC is the company through which I consult—nothing more and nothing less. I mention it because a lot of the consulting I've done over the years has contributed to many of the lessons described here.

Enough about me. I listed a lot of valuable lessons I learned along the way. I hope you now feel more comfortable with what I have to say. Now let's dig deeper.

CHAPTER 2

Innovation, Entrepreneurialism, and Commercialization

Innovation is not commercialization. Entrepreneurs exploit innovation for commercial purposes. They're the scavengers of the innovation process. Sure, they sometimes invent, but by and large, they convert the work of others into profitable products and services.

Here's one for the ages (Roos, 2021): we're told that Bill Gates and Steve Ballmer did not write MS-DOS. They bought it for $50K and then licensed it to IBM. We're also told that they didn't write Internet Explorer. We're told that they licensed the software from Spyglass and based three versions of Explorer on the original code. Obviously, Microsoft did extremely well commercializing the inventions of others and is a near-perfect example of how innovation precedes commercialization and how entrepreneurs exploit both.

Who are you? Do you invent or commercialize? Maybe a little bit of both? It's important to see yourself for what you really are and behave accordingly. Did Gates ever acknowledge that he did not *invent* MS-DOS? (He did.) Does it really matter? Not to the outside world, for sure, but internally, it matters more than you might appreciate. Innovation is personal, so make sure you give credit where credit's due. Scientists and technologists are extremely sensitive about recognition. Remember that when you're carving up equity.

Why is all this so important?

- *Because entrepreneurs should have exquisite innovation and commercialization radar*. They should constantly search for innovative ideas they can exploit. This is a skillset that many entrepreneurs do not have. Do you have it? Do you know where innovation lives? Do you have relationships with universities, corporate centers of excellence, industry research and development teams, and superstars who can source innovation? If you don't, you need to build them.

- Never forget the mistake I made with asynchronous learning networks (ALN). I had an opportunity to commercialize some of the ALN technology but failed. ***Fine-tune your commercialization radar right now.***

Most of the companies in my professional orbit were founded by entrepreneurs who exploited the creative work of others—which is fine because the skill sets of innovators and entrepreneurs are completely different.

Innovation

So, what *is* innovation? How many different definitions and categories of innovation are there? Scholars and practitioners continue to torture the concept in search of definitions they hope everyone will accept. Here are just a few from our friends at Wikipedia:

> Innovation is the multistage process whereby organizations transform ideas into new/improved products, service or processes, in order to advance, compete and differentiate themselves successfully in their marketplace

> Disruptive innovation in contrast refers to a process by which a new product or service creates a new market (e.g., transistor radio, free crowdsourced encyclopedia), eventually displacing established competitors.

> Incremental innovation ... refines and extends an established design. Improvement occurs in individual components, but the

underlying core design concepts, and the links between them, remain the same.

This is a deliberate example of analysis paralysis where one might easily get stuck analyzing and selecting just the right definition of innovation for their purposes—which is what we'll avoid here. Innovation has certain features important to the start-up process. So, for our purposes here, we'll define innovation this way:

- Innovation is the creation of a value-added method, tool, technique, or technology that impacts the way problems are defined, framed, and solved.

Innovation lives in a matrix, as Figure 2.1 suggests. ***There are three distinct kinds of innovation: incremental innovation, innovation that results from modernization, and disruptive innovation.*** The three kinds are applied to products, services, business processes, and whole business models across multiple vertical industries. Study Figure 2.1.

Most *innovation* is boring—anything but disruptive. In fact, it's not innovation at all. Most of the companies where I've worked love to exaggerate their innovation chops. Most of them disrupt by accident, context, and opportunity. Amazon started selling books. We met with Jeff Bezos in the 1990s at Safeguard while he was raising money for his *ecommerce* book site—which is all he talked about. The rest is history. (No, we did not invest.)

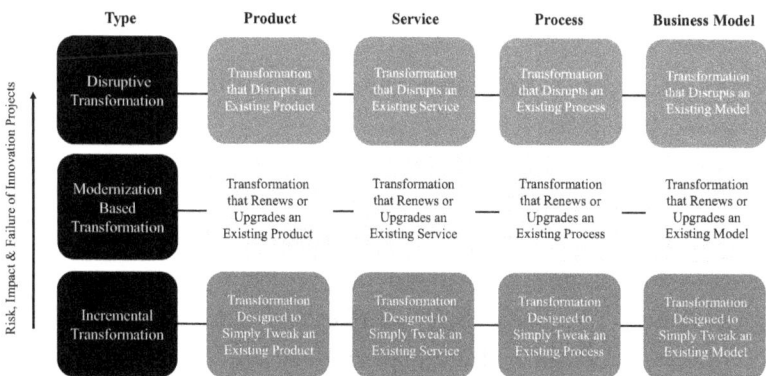

Type	Product	Service	Process	Business Model
Disruptive Transformation	Transformation that Disrupts an Existing Product	Transformation that Disrupts an Existing Service	Transformation that Disrupts an Existing Process	Transformation that Disrupts an Existing Model
Modernization Based Transformation	Transformation that Renews or Upgrades an Existing Product	Transformation that Renews or Upgrades an Existing Service	Transformation that Renews or Upgrades an Existing Process	Transformation that Renews or Upgrades an Existing Model
Incremental Transformation	Transformation Designed to Simply Tweak an Existing Product	Transformation Designed to Simply Tweak an Existing Service	Transformation Designed to Simply Tweak an Existing Process	Transformation Designed to Simply Tweak an Existing Model

Risk, Impact & Failure of Innovation Projects

Figure 2.1 Types and targets of innovation

Disruptive innovation is hard and usually evolves from incremental innovation. Sometimes it just lands on us, like Oculus did at Facebook. But that's generally not the case.

Takeaways?

- Be careful how you define your innovation—unless you're pitching to people who don't care. Note also that innovation can hit different markets in different ways. Are you innovating a product? A service? A process? Or an entire business model? Think about Uber, Airbnb, and VRBO. How did they disrupt the transportation and vacation industries? Did they disrupt a process, a business model, or just a service? Or everything? For example, what will happen to the home generator market when people can power their homes from their EVs?

- Do the dance. Thread the needle. Investors crave disruptive innovation because unicorn money is possible primarily through disruptive innovation. But the number of ideas that are truly disruptive is small. LiquidHub made a fortune selling services that were *traditional* by any definition. Read the room (and the times). Who wants to hear what? Match expectations with messaging. If the audience wants to hear about innovation, serve some up (but not too much). If it's OK with something less, serve that up. Your call. You get the idea.

Entrepreneurialism

Entrepreneurialism *exploits* innovation. Here's a definition that suits our purposes (Wikipedia):

Entrepreneurship is the creation or extraction of value. With this definition, entrepreneurship is viewed as change, generally entailing risk beyond what is normally encountered in starting a business ... (others) have described entrepreneurship as the process of designing, launching, and running a new business, which is often similar to a small business, or as the capacity and willingness to develop, organize, and manage a business venture along with any of its risks to make a profit.

This definition will do just fine. The focus is on **the exploitation of innovation for commercial purposes** through entrepreneurialism. Ideally, these commercial purposes are achieved through the creation, launch, and growth of a new company followed by a successful exit. But everyone knows that most startups fail, which is why this analysis is important to entrepreneurs and the investors who fund them.

Commercialization

Entrepreneurs convert innovative product and service ideas—really hypotheses—into product and service MVPs—minimum viable products—that can be tested by the market.

More formally (Kenton, 2020):

> Commercialization is the process of bringing new products or services to market. The broader act of commercialization entails production, distribution, marketing, sales, customer support, and other key functions critical to achieving the commercial success of the new product or service.

The exploitation of innovation for commercial purposes is where this book lives, as suggested in Figure 2.2. It's a simple view of the relationship between innovation and commercialization enabled by entrepreneurialism. It's a clean way to think about processes, just a graphic worth thinking about—not a step-by-step requirement. This

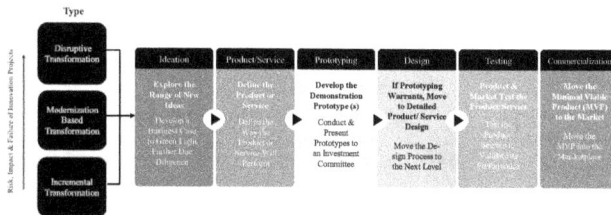

Figure 2.2 Innovation to commercialization through entrepreneurialism

distinction is important. Way too many entrepreneurs become addicted to methodological purity, which slows the commercialization process down to the point where too few MVPs come out of the pipeline.

The best entrepreneurs find rocket scientists with amazing ideas. They then figure out how to convert the technology to products and services through a business model that brings the product or service to market. In short, the best entrepreneurs know how to commercialize—all as described by Figure 2.2.

Soft Versus Hard Methodology

There are natural tensions among *methodology*, innovation, entrepreneurialism, and commercialization. Some entrepreneurs *manage* the innovation and commercialization processes tightly—***way too tightly***—so be careful not to strangle innovation, entrepreneurialism, or commercialization with methodology that **requires** *steps* be taken before something is declared innovative or commercializable. There are often committees and task forces that must decide if something has satisfied all of the investment criteria before any innovative ideas can proceed. What am I talking about?

Phase-gating, for example, is a terrific methodology that helps vet ideas, products, and services as they evolve toward market readiness (Wikipedia):

A phase-gate process (also referred to as a waterfall process) is a project management technique in which an initiative or project (e.g., new product development, software development, process improvement, business change) is divided into distinct *stages* or *phases*, separated by decision points (known as *gates*).

At each gate, continuation is decided by (typically) a manager, steering committee, or governance board. The decision is made based on forecasts and information available at the time, including the business case, risk analysis, and availability of necessary resources (e.g., money, people with correct competencies).

MVPs are the objective (see Figure 2.2).

What's an MVP (Agile Alliance, 2024)? It's a *new* product ready for market testing to determine if the product (or service) has longer-term legs, that is, if the product (or service) can scale because the market wants it.

Remember that phase-gating can take on a life unto itself (Wikipedia):

> One problem with the phase-gate process is the potential for structural organization to interfere with creativity and innovation, as overly structured processes may cause creativity to be reduced in importance and to hinder the largely iterative process of innovation.

Balance is key here. Methodology—including phase-gating—is always ***conceptually*** powerful. But make sure it never becomes a stranglehold on commercialization. I've seen companies hide behind methodology as a conscious or unconscious response to risk management. ***Make sure methodology never assumes a life unto itself, and make sure the methodological gurus never take over the process.*** (This happens, for example, when Agile software development trainers take over the software development process—which has been known to happen!)

Innovation is part Wild, Wild West, and part ballet. It's not an ERP project. Entrepreneurs should know when they should shoot and when they should dance, but they should never become reactive to methods, tools, and techniques because someone once upon a time described an innovation process.

Is there a defined, repeatable process here that can be tamed by methodologies? ***No—and there never was:***

- One of the greatest myths of the start-up process is the utility of methodological templates, or any preordained formulae, that require entrepreneurs to answer a checklist of questions before launching a business or seeking funding. Anyone can answer a checklist of questions—but the answers are always temporary! Methodological templates are *OK* but never definitive.

- ***Please do not ignore this lesson: innovation, entrepreneurialism, and commercialization are not predictable or schedulable.*** Innovation is opportunistically pursued by informed, relentless individuals with solid teams—and relationships—who have the financial means to follow a dream ***that's in every respect a hypothesis about what might—or might not—work.***

- *Templates* are designed by people who need structure and order to understand what entrepreneurs are trying to do—even when the entrepreneurs themselves cannot always describe their ideas cleanly or consistently.

- ***Investors and their due diligence consultants are the largest consumers of methodologies.*** So, if you want their money, you must use some *pitching aids*. You must be two people, of two minds. You should already know there's no way to predict technology breakthroughs, market demand, or competitive pressures. They're discovered along the way. But you must act like they're controllable because your investors are often incapable of understanding real innovation or entrepreneurial processes, especially if they've never actually created anything new in their careers.

- Never tell unsophisticated investors that you have no idea what your technology team will discover or what the competition might do. You need to explain your goals. So learn how to time travel between alternative universes. (Remember the importance of the ability to kind of, sort of, *fake*?)

Moving Targets

Entrepreneurial events occur all the time. They're seldom wrapped in boxes with labeled processes. ***They're random, opportunistic hypotheses that require testing in the marketplace of funding and sales—and make no mistake, these two marketplaces have nothing in common.***

Lessons?

- Empirical market research may love an idea, and investors may hate the same one. Unless the actual market embraces the idea (with sales) before investors decide what to do. Of course, when that happens, the investment price goes up, though you'd be hard pressed to find an investor willing to happily pay full value for validated market interest, even if there's growing, profitable revenue. Very few have consistent visions based on a solid understanding of technology or business trends, **which means that most investors are valuation challenged, which means their default practice is to discount valuations for whatever reasons they can find (and some they can't).**

- At the end of the day, as an entrepreneur seeking money, you set the initial valuation to which your investors will react. The most aggressive reactions will come from disciplined Angels and institutional investors (like PEVCs). Remember that if you want their money, you will have to listen to their ideas, challenge their valuation models, and inspect the terms of the investment they might make. Valuation is the most important initial fight you will have with investors. Prepare to make strong operational arguments **but even stronger strategic ones**. (There's more on valuation later.)

All good, but never forget:

- A key lesson for innovators and entrepreneurs is simple: those with the most gold make the rules.
- **Networks of personal and professional relationships—also called ecosystems or Keiretsus—explain much more about success than anything else.** No kidding: height, hair, and teeth are also predictors. Pedigrees from the right colleges, universities, and country clubs help a lot. Graduate degrees from the right colleges and universities also help, especially since they come with their own ecosystems and Keiretsus. Make sure to account for all this when starting a company, raising money and monetizing your hard work.

What about intelligence, due diligence, and hard work? Of course, they're important—but they're not independent predictors of success:

- In fact, an entrepreneur's probability of success is as dependent upon his or her personal and professional relationships as it is on intelligence and commitment—not just market conditions, which can derail momentum as quickly as it appears.

Most entrepreneurs could never work at American Airlines, Xfinity, or Cigna without losing their minds. The corporate structure and professional expectations would choke them to death. They need the imprecision, chaos, and unpredictability of the start-up world—even if they refuse to admit it (more on that later). They also need control—even if they have no idea what they're doing. For many entrepreneurs, chaos grants control, ***even when they're the source of the chaos, especially if they're the source of capital.***

If you find yourself yearning for stability, consistency, and predictability, you might want to rethink your mission—and stop reading this book.

CHAPTER 3

Technology Trends and Opportunities

If you're a digital entrepreneur, it obviously helps to understand technology trends, especially because many of your investors probably won't have a clue: *someone must assess—and communicate—the uniqueness of your products and services and the markets you intend to attack. That someone should be you*. (If you're good at it. If you're not, you need to find a persuasive spokesperson.)

There are several levels of understanding here. The first is about trends and trajectories that will persist for decades. A level below looks at trends that will unfold in the next three to five years. All entrepreneurs should understand short- and longer-term trends if they want their business models and whole business strategies to succeed. Some of these trends are short *and* longer term, such as automation enabled by artificial intelligence (AI), machine learning (ML), and especially generative AI (Gen AI). The broad application of artificial general intelligence (AGI) will lag.

Trends spell opportunity, opportunity spells profit, profit spells valuation and valuation spells exit. Pay attention to trends. They can be the sources of commercialization or dovetail with other trends that amplify your products or services.

Lesson?

- Tracking trends is a start-up prerequisite. You cannot create new products or services unless you know what's happening out there. You can outsource this or develop your own tracking methodology. I strongly recommend that you develop your own trends tracking team.

Here are some trends you must track—for now.

Trends

Think about exploiting these six technology macro trends right now:

- Automation
- Low-code platforms
- Sustainability applications
- Data lakes/fabrics/architectures
- Augmented and virtual reality
- AI, ML, and GenAI

Automation

We've not even begun to define the range of processes that will be automated in 10 years. ***Suffice it to say that today what humans do will be widely replaced by software applications and robotics.*** (Avoid silly debates about how humans will always be necessary because they won't always be necessary.) The short list of replaceable professions? Auditors, manufacturers, lawyers, diagnosticians, salespersons, teachers, marketers, programmers, researchers, writers, couriers, customer servicers, food preparation, and drivers among what Goldman Sachs says could be 300 million jobs (Vallance, 2023). The precise number of jobs that will be automated—***eliminated***—is impossible to predict, but the trends are inevitable. How many companies see their business processes and whole business models as automation candidates? Is this your vision? How about these?

- In 10 years, there will be self-driving cars and trucks everywhere. Few of us will actually own cars, especially those who live in crowded urban or suburban areas. By 2035, automobile accidents will have declined dramatically. The whole notion of *insurance* will be redefined.
- Dead entertainers will tour the country; *concerts* will be physical and virtual.

- No one will prepare a tax return.
- No one will stand in line to vote.
- No one will go anywhere to buy anything (unless they really want to).
- Many of us will only travel virtually. If you can't go to the Louvre and stare at the Mona Lisa (for your allotted few minutes), you will *see* it for as long as you like with floating data about every aspect of its creation. Same for all of the travel destinations we've been conditioned to desire.
- Commuting—and traffic wars—will be optional. More than half of us will work from home.
- Students will learn from wherever, whenever. Learning will be immersed, experiential, and remote—and be personalized to what we already know, our learning styles, our progress, and immediate and longer-term requirements.
- Campuses will be where undergraduate students socialize, though socialization will occur from video immersion as often as it does through fraternities and sororities. Graduate students will network virtually; elite schools will maintain in-person education and networking.
- Training will be virtual.
- Sensors (everywhere) will know what we need and want and execute transactions automatically.
- It's impossible to forget a birthday or anniversary—or wonder what gifts to buy.
- Our homes and offices will be very smart and get smarter by watching us do everything we do—all the time.
- We'll browse digital catalogs from headsets (and eventually contact lenses) as small and as fashionable as the sunglasses everyone wants. Heads-up displays will be everywhere.
- In spite of what banks tells us today, money will be gone by 2035. All transactions will be digital. Cash is long gone; alternative currencies are alive and well. Not just cryptocurrency but exchanges where digital commodities—like nonfungible

tokens (NFTs)—will compete with traditional and alternative currencies.

- 3D manufacturing and printing will power tiny home factories where we'll produce a lot of what we need around the house.
- Unless information is regulated, misinformation and disinformation will wreak social, economic, and political havoc on even the most stable governments. Social media platforms will generate deep fakes and other threats at unimaginable paces. Bot wars will be out of control.
- Full immersion will forever change the way we watch—and experience—sports.
- Online sports gambling will be highly regulated. Maybe. It depends on how much damage it does to families.
- Many of us will be chipped by 2035. We'll be able to buy things, access currency, enter our homes, and start our cars without keys, cards, or smartphones. Small chips will reside between our thumbs and index fingers. We won't even know they're there unless we pinch ourselves.
- Cyberwarfare will be continuous, lethal and commonplace.
- People will lose their jobs, and while the number of new digital jobs will grow, there will be an education and training gap in how we prepare for those jobs—despite all the educational technology that will be *floating* around.

The drivers of all this change are already out of the barn. By 2035, 10G will connect everything. AI will enable just about everything from recognizing fruit and vegetables ready for picking by robotic arms to self-driving cars that know how avoid people crossing streets and read ambiguous construction signs. Computer vision, image recognition, natural language understanding, and algorithms—all sorts of algorithms—will enable 2035. The Internet-of-Everything—IoE—will add billions of devices to the world's networks. 3D modeling and manufacturing will construct cars, houses, and boats. Augmented and virtual reality will transform entertainment, commerce, and learning. Robots will perform dangerous tasks, pick fruit, flip hamburgers, check us into hotels, provide child care, and comfort the lonely. By 2035, many of us will be fully immersed in shared spaces that merge our physical and virtual existences. Imagine the impact on gaming, entertainment, commerce, marketing, communication, and relationships. The metaverse—which will actually exist in 2035—is where all the trends come together—for better or worse. The distinction between real and virtual will blur.

Do you understand these trends? There's incalculable amounts of money that can be made from them.

Low-Code Platforms

Programming, as we understand it today, will disappear in less than a decade (except the programming necessary to develop low-code and no-code platforms—which will also disappear as GenAI platforms learn how to write the code that will run the code). Does this mean programming will completely disappear? Almost, but it does mean that huge parts of applications development will be on low-code/no-code platforms by *developers* with no formal programming training.

It's impossible to overstate the impact of low-code/no-code platforms—and now AI chatbots—which enable nonprogrammers to develop applications. Your low-code team can develop applications faster and more cost-effectively than traditional requirements-driven programming-based application development.

You need low-code/no-code/AI chatbot jockeys. Expand low-code expertise way beyond the technology department and spread it across your business analysts. ***But also note that the entire development world has already been turned on its head with GenAI and the low-code platforms that enable the development of AI, ML, and GenAI applications.*** Track this trend more closely than any of the others (see below for much more on AI, machine learning and Generative AI).

Sustainability

The partnership between Google and mCloud Technologies makes the point: the marriage between digital technology and sustainability has officially been consummated. This partnership will result in applications that will, among other things, impact our survival. Even the United Nations is focused on *"achieving environmental sustainability with digital technology."*

But attention to sustainability includes much more. Step 1? Determine the clusters you need. Are your products and services sustainability-ready? Are there opportunities you've yet to consider? Google and mCloud will focus on *"sustainability apps aimed at curbing carbon emissions worldwide,"* including oil and gas, buidlings and wind.

Do you manufacture anything? Do you ship products in containers? Do you deliver anything? What applications connected to your products and services supply chain should be re-engineered? The development and application of sustainability hardware and software is exploding. Consumers are ready to adopt applications that enable sustainability (Brown, 2022).

Data Architecture, Data Lakes, and Data Fabrics

Data is still king. Or as it's been described by the AI community, the new oil. You need a real plan here. In the 20th century, we had databases, which became data warehouses that are now data lakes optimized through data fabrics. Because most data is unstructured, you have no choice but to build data lakes under the guidance of data fabrics, which all includes an enterprise data architecture.

Architecturally, companies want a data infrastructure that enables flexible data analytics and data-driven applications development. Companies are rethinking enterprise architecture away from the hamburger pictures of the 20th century and see it as a proactive blueprint.

Data lakes are nondiscriminatory data repositories that enable data analytics of all kinds of data. Data fabrics speak to an overall analytics philosophy. Data architectures are the guidance, governance, and glue. Can you help with the evolution of all-things-data? ***Can you use GenAI to do these things?*** There's a lot of money here.

Augmented and Virtual Reality

Augmented and virtual reality technologies are still growing (though not as fast as the hype around them). Apple entered the headset race with Vision Pro. Microsoft is landing massive HoloLens deals with the U.S. military (Sag, 2021). The gaming industry is fully committed (Fortune, 2021), and there's no metaverse – whenever it finally arrives – without AR/VR (Levy, 2021). Like many of the clusters, AR/VR technology has enormous potential, even in industries we don't immediately associate with AR/VR. Should you be in the AR/VR education, travel, entertainment, gaming, retail, and healthcare industries? Who on your team is fully immersed in this technology?

AI, Machine Learning, and Generative AI

AI, ML, and especially GenAI are the most important business technologies in a generation. The applications of AI/ML/GenAI to business models and processes are endless. AI/ML/GenAI focus on the automation of business processes and tasks, intelligent decision-making, predictive analytics, personalization, and conversational interfaces, among many other areas. There's narrow AI/ML and generalized AI/ML which refers to the boundability of problems. Most problems are well-bounded problems, that is, problems that can be modeled. For example, automating the processes by which someone should receive a loan, or whether someone should be admitted to a university, can be modeled quite easily, because the variables that predict to accept/reject are known. GenAI enables the creation of new information across vertical industries and business functions.

Takeaway?

- *You need a dedicated team to assess AI start-up opportunities.*

Let's dig deeper into AI, ML, GenAI, and AGI because there's so much opportunity—and a little fear—here. Entrepreneurs must chase the hottest technology for obvious reasons, but intelligent systems technology is different from the other game-changers we've seen over the years.

It's as significant as the internet, or as Jamie Dimon, the CEO of JPMorganChase suggests, as significant as electricity.

If AI has such potential, we must all stop denying the impact it will have on the professions. Despite the chorus that AI has clear limits, AI cannot make the kinds of decisions humans are uniquely qualified to make, will always have limitations, will continue to hallucinate (though over time even these will disappear), and will not replace managers,[*] AI will decimate many professions, and in the process, create opportunities for new business models. The general conclusion that humans and their uniqueness need not worry too much about losing their jobs to algorithms—and AI will remain assistants rather than partners and certainly not bosses—is flat out wrong.

Let's remember that AI (ML and especially GenAI) is very new. We're at Step 1 of a 10-step journey where the 10th step is always moving. No one knows how this will end, except that it won't—which is why judgments about which jobs are resilient and which aren't today are, by definition, misleading. How could thought leaders possibly know the power of AI 10 or 20 years from now or what professions—many of which have yet to be invented—will grow, shrink, or disappear altogether? How could pundits possibly know how this story ends?

It's impossible to talk about the role that AI will play without segmentation. We need a matrix of domains and timelines. Some domains, like medical imaging, will yield to ML and GenAI faster than others. Which are which? The nature of problems and work must also be

---

[*] The *Harvard Business Review* is leading the charge with a suite of articles that insist AI will not replace human decision makers and that AI "will enable knowledge workers to concentrate on value-adding activities where human expertise is indispensable" (Senz, 2023). De Cremer and Kasparov (2021) argue that "AI should augment human intelligence, not replace it." Martela and Luoma (2021) flat out declare that "AI will never replace managers" because humans are better at *reframing* problems than machines—at least for now. Other papers in the *Harvard Business Review* suggest that too much focus on AI can actually cause *more problems than it's solving* (Acar, 2024), and Shrier et al. (2023) describe the jobs most and least affected by AI with the simple title "is your job AI resilient?" Finally, Lakhani (2023) argues that "AI won't replace humans—but humans with AI will replace humans without AI."

specified. Well-bounded domains, regardless of their complexity, are all fair game.

Gemini tells us that *"generative AI ... excels in tasks that involve creating new data, often creative in nature. Here are some problem domains where generative AI shines: image and video generation, content creation, data augmentation and drug discovery."*

I recently made the argument that higher education and the staff that enables it are all in the crosshairs of AI. These predictions are based upon the tasks that professors and students perform to learn, and how the domain of higher education can be modeled around processes that are ***today*** particularly amenable to AI tools. Higher education is not the only vulnerable domain. Domains with similar well-bounded processes are also targets.

It's time to stop reassuring ourselves about what AI will not replace. If the technology trends are any indication of impact, ML, GenAI, and AGI are far more likely to replace than preserve knowledge workers. It will take some time for this prediction to be validated or rejected, but arguments that AI has clear limits, and that humans are uniquely qualified to make certain decisions are wrong. While it's impossible to know what happens in 10 years, we can be sure that AI will replace a growing number of knowledge workers in the next three to five years.

The Case of Higher Education

Let's assume that you're teaching a course. Now let's assume that you're taking a course or have enrolled in a degree program. Let's also assume that you know something about GenAI, which many professors and lots more students already do. Let's also assume that GenAI tools will become incredibly smarter, better, and faster, which is the easiest prediction anyone can make. If all of these assumptions are true, what happens to higher education?

Have we missed something huge here?

We sure have.

If fact, it's so big that it literally changes the very premise of learning as we know it today. It's astonishing that most professors, administrators, and even donors don't see the proverbial train barreling down the tracks, perhaps like how climate deniers cannot calculate storms, rainfall, fires, floods, droughts, and unbearable summers. Maybe it's just a repeat of the Luddite phenomenon that surrounds the adoption of any new technology. Who knows, but worse, many universities have actually banned GenAI, which is a naïve attempt to regulate a technology more compelling than the Internet, and in so doing, have actually provided encouragement to faculty and administrators to pretend that GenAI and its CustomGPT children are more of a threat than a service. Further, faculty who have not used GenAI to develop and deliver courses have already missed an extraordinary opportunity to improve the learning process for their students and increase the learning outcomes of their courses.

As a professor of business technology, I have begun to treat GenAI and CustomGPTs as willing teaching assistants only to discover that they're much closer to partners than assistants. I have asked Gemini and ChatGPT (and others) to develop syllabi and then compared them with my own as a way to improve my courses. Gemini and Chat have often made terrific suggestions and found materials I missed in what I thought was an exhaustive search. Selected CustomGPTs also summarize huge amounts of text, website content, and even videos, which also helps enormously. Next step: use CustomGPTs to create course videos from textual or spoken requirements, which will be especially helpful for fully online courses—in multiple domains and languages. NotebookLM is now of course a member of the same family.

Course Design and Development

Let's start with a course—a graduate course for our purposes here—in marketing. Many professors in the not too distant past—and definitely even today—develop their syllabi by converting research and knowledge (and sometimes even actual experience) into what they believe represent marketing principles, cases, and best practices with a wide variety of readings, content, videos, and so on. Textbooks are still used as the field itself—all fields—evolve faster than publication schedules and where many academics still frown upon applied versus theoretical research. If the truth be told, professors cannot possibly track all of the basic and applied research in marketing (or any field) published across the globe, in spite of what Google Scholar says. Few have the time to read all of this research. That said, and of course depending on the professor, traditional, unassisted courses can generate some useful learning outcomes.

But what about now?

Let's look at how large language models can develop a syllabus with detailed prompts like this:

Develop a syllabus for a marketing course for graduate students that covers the fundamental principles of marketing, marketing cases, readings that include some theory and practice—with an emphasis on practice—with requirements that include projects, essays, tests and in-class conversations that illuminate theory and practice. Also develop lecture notes for me with bullet points—derived from the readings—that will focus the students class-by-class on the right topics. Please also assume that the class is 15 weeks long with readings, assignments, and five salient topics (captured in the bullet points) per week. Use only current readings: nothing older that 2020. I'd also like some learning outcomes I should expect the course to generate.

If you doubt the power of GenAI, prompt Gemini with the preceding prompt and then follow-up with: *"please provide a longer list of readings including articles and books as well as links to web sites that support the course."*

Play with Gemini a little more by asking: *"please identify some online company and YouTube videos that can be used each week."*

By the way, I did all this in less than three minutes. Anyone can. (Imagine what could be developed in 30.)

What about course videos? Professors can create them (by lecturing into a camera for several hours) from the readings, from their interpretations of the readings, from their own case experiences—from anything they like. But now, professors can direct the creation of the videos by talking—actually describing—what they'd like the video to communicate with their or another image. Wait. What? They can make a video by talking to a tool and even select the image they want the actor to use? Yes. They can also add a British accent and insert some (GenAI-developed) jokes into the videos if they like. All this and much more is now pretty easy—with avatars. This means that a professor can specify how long the video should be, what sources should be consulted, and describe the demeanor the professor wants to project.

This only touches the surface of what professors can do with GenAI and CustomGPTs to create courses with everything—and a whole lot more—they need or want to teach a great marketing course, which fundamentally changes the way courses are conceived, designed, developed, and delivered in higher education today. Did I forget the cases? Introduce a product and then ask Gemini to write the press release and describe the marketing campaign. If that's a student assignment, it only takes minutes to complete the task.

It's gets worse—or better, depending on one's perspective. Many professors assign readings and then discuss them in class. But what if the readings were summarized and then interpreted by GenAI? What if— and hopefully this isn't the case today—a professor wanted a PowerPoint presentation generated from the readings (not textbook readings—they already come with dated PowerPoints). No, I'm talking about random readings—maybe even something professors wanted the students to immediately read or watch—like something about Superbowl ads or the endless stream of Ozempic commercials. Yes, regardless of its source or format, it could be summarized, interpreted, and packaged for presentation without any professorial touch.

What's a "Professor"?

With all this power, what's the unique contribution professors can really make? Arguments are made all the time about how effective classroom experiences can be, that there's something special about human-to-human contact in the learning process.

Everyone likes to reassure professors that they'll always be necessary, but will they? It may be that accreditation boards will save them from what otherwise is inevitable—which is replacement along some assist/

partner/replace continuum over a period of time, but no later than 2035. Gemini has already reduced their contributions to a three-minute waltz.

What happens when syllabi are easily better than anything professors could design or develop? When, for example, will GenAI read MRIs faster and better than radiologists? Conduct more accurate breast examinations? Admit/reject students to colleges and universities? There are trends here that cannot be ignored. It's all just around the corner.

Professors are not a protected species.

What about when more and more courses move online? Professors who teach online are barely there anyway, right? You'd think that it would occur to university professors who "host" online courses today that they're demonstrating how unnecessary they are to the learning process. They develop syllabi, identify content, develop (or appropriate someone else's) videos, identify assignments and tests—all of which we've already demonstrated can today be enabled by GenAI. Fully asynchronous students often have little or no human contact with actual professors. How does all that demonstrate necessity?

GenAI can develop curricula and deliver courses—content, videos, exams, and so on—without any human touch. In fact, while accreditation boards would never approve, it's absolutely possible to automate the entire asynchronous online education process with GenAI, avatars and CustomGPTs. Professors would then nod approval (for the sake of accreditation) of the courses they do not create and the grades they no longer give. Crazy? Not at all. In fact, it's possible right now.

Students and GenAI

Let's take the content and the requirements of the course—the video lectures, readings, research reports, websites, and essay examinations—and match these activities with GenAI. First, students do not need to read or watch anything. Let's say that again: students do not need to read or watch anything—unless their professor takes roll—*even if their professor takes roll*. Instead, they can rely upon summarizers and converters to reduce their workload. If they choose to avoid summarizers and converters, they can hire GenAI tutors to see how well they're doing and suggest how they might improve their performance. Regardless, they no longer have to read articles, inspect websites, immerse themselves in textbooks, write essays, or take tests. All they have to do is ask NotebookLM (or other tools) for help.

With the help of GenAI/CustomGPTs, online students actually have very little to do. Summaries of everything are easily generated, and student requirements are almost as easily satisfied. They too don't need to read or watch anything. In completely asynchronous courses, no one even checks, even if videos can determine if they've been watched. In fact, students may appear to have read and watched everything—as evidenced in the tests they take—when they've barely bonded with course materials.

What's a "Student"?

When students have all this help, what's their role in the learning process? First, let's assume they will use all the help they can find because it's unlikely students will reject ways to learn faster and easier. Part-time students will especially appreciate shortcuts, because they're on a different educational clock than full-time students— who will also accept the help. But it's not at all clear how learning outcomes will be measured, unless learning outcome metrics are exchanged for others, like speed/ease-to-degree-completion. For students, the assignment is to understand the relationship between real versus surrogacy and how *engagement* should be defined—that ends with an *A* for the course.

Now What?

Academia's response to all this has been uneven. On the one hand, universities are warning—and punishing—students who use GenAI tools to satisfy course requirements. But on the other hand, they're teaching the technology where students are required to use GenAI to satisfy course requirements. It's pretty quiet about how it expects faculty to deal with GenAI, "Light" Language Models and and CustomGPTs.

There's no question that academia's response is late, inconsistent, and incomplete. The world of CustomGPTs has acerbated the challenge, as more and more special-purpose education applications help faculty and students reduce their contributions to the learning process.

A wide open question: *"who does what?"* Another one: *"why are professors compensated the way they are when their digital assistants and partners do much of the work?"* And lastly, *"how can anyone measure learning outcomes when they're contrived by GenAI?"*

Higher education needs a fast audit. The roles that professors and students should play in the education process must be redefined—and then reinvented, if not reimagined altogether. The larger issue is the relationship between humans and AI. It's essential that professors and students understand how to work with increasingly intelligent machines that will evolve from teaching assistants, to faculty partners and eventually to curriculum bosses, and how faculty will share—and eventually yield—decision-making and problem-solving power over time. As suggested, students will define their roles as team members where courses are taken by themselves, Gemini/Chat/Copilot/and so on, and a long list of CustomGPTs. The educational process will be crowded, a far cry from the old teacher-student model some believe still defines the educational process.

Accreditors and credentialists must immediately rewrite the rules as GenAI becomes a major player in the educational process. It's a GenAI/faculty/student threesome now—and forever. Watch as the differences among correspondence, distance learning, and online programs shrink to nothing—and the expanding role GenAI will play in the process as the regulators of correspondence, distance learning, and online programs struggle with the merger. The same process will play out in the classroom where roles will also be redefined, reinvented, and re-imagined.

At the end of the day, it's an exercise in the reallocation of educational power, accountability, standards, and compensation.

Key? The definition of *academic engagement* will have to change as the role of GenAI/CustomGPTs explodes. Just look at five parts of academic engagement as defined by the Code of Federal Regulations:

Attending a synchronous class, lecture, recitation, or field or laboratory activity, physically or online, where there is an opportunity for interaction between the instructor and students …

Submitting an academic assignment …

Taking an assessment or an exam …

Participating in an interactive tutorial, webinar, or other interactive computer-assisted instruction …

Participating in a study group, group project, or an online discussion that is assigned by the institution; or … interacting with an instructor about academic matters …

GenAI will forever change the definition of student/machine engagement (CustomGPT.ai, 2024)—which it already has.

Now What?

Some universities will just keep their heads in the sand for as long as they can, often with unrealistic punitive policies about GenAI as a growing number of their students use ChatGPT, Gemini, and other tools to summarize, convert, write, research, and take tests, among many other class tasks.

Other universities—the smart ones—will immediately assemble open-minded task forces to explore how and where GenAI will impact higher education. A few innovative ones—like MIT—will immediately pilot aspects of automation to determine what parts of the education process can be in-sourced, co-sourced, and outsourced. They will most likely conduct this experiment with online courses where the possibility and taste for automation is the greatest.

Finally, universities should proactively engage with those who accredit educational programs to push them toward defining how engagement and other activities should be defined as GenAI moves from assistants to partners and beyond.

This use case demonstrates how "AI" will impact education and training. There are so many other examples to consider.

How to Track Business-Technology Trends

Beyond AI, machine learning and Generative AI, there are other technologies that entrepreneurs must track. I've always used a macro/ enabling/market trends-driven model to identify and validate technology trends. Some macro trends are relatively easy to identify. Examples? Messaging-to-buying, cloud computing, mobile everything, automation, alternative realities, and digital security. Others include location-based services, intelligent systems, digital entertainment, wearables, and analytics-for-everyone. You must understand these macro trends—and the start-up opportunities they enable.

Today, there are many professionals who use their own methods, tools, and techniques to understand where technology trajectories are

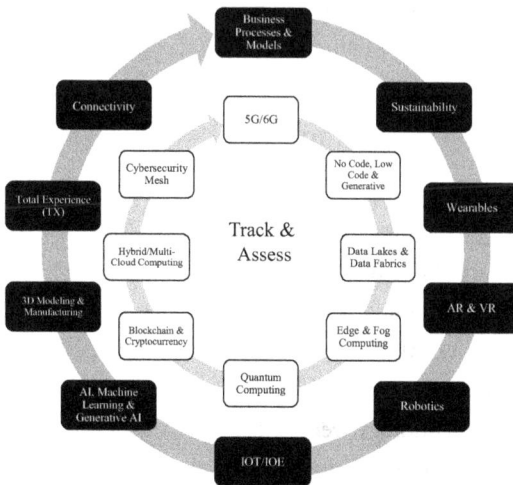

Figure 3.1 Emerging technology opportunities

The range of infrastructure and application technologies available to entrepreneurs.

going and how to profit from the development and application of macro and enabling technologies. Annual forecasts by industry analysts like the Gartner Group and the major consultancies can help a lot, but at the end of the day, it's the responsibility of entrepreneurs to understand macro and enabling trends and how they might be monetized. Oh, and lets' not forget our new partners—Claude, Gemini, Llama, Chat, and all the rest. They can track technology trends as efficiently as anyone. In fact, I recently compared the lists of strategic technology trends generated by the usual pundits with what the large language models (LLMs) generated. You can guess who won.

The technologies we track today—recognizing that the list will change over time—appear in Figure 3.1. Note that there are infrastructure technologies in the inner circle and applications technologies in the outer circle.

We're also tracking GenAI more closely than most of the technologies on our list because this technology represents a sea change that will unleash the greatest profit engine in history as expensive human-managed processes are replaced by cheaper and more efficient digital ones. What we've seen to date from bots and applications like ChatGPT, Gemini, Claude, Llama, Midjourney, and Synthesia (and so many others) is just the beginning of how AI/ML/GenAI will transform business processes and whole business models, which is why companies should invest heavily in intelligent systems technology.

Implications?

- Technology entrepreneurs—*you*—must understand macro and enabling technology trends as well as the M&A activity that accelerates and validates the trends. You need to locate your innovative technology with specific reference to competing technologies. At the same time, do not expect investors, bankers, or lawyers to understand much of anything about macro or enabling technology trends. They will, however, know something about M&A transactions, because their teams track technology transactions that affect their ability to exit their investments.

- If you're an entrepreneur incapable of understanding macro and enabling technology trends, then you're not an authentic technology entrepreneur. You will need to surround yourself with technologists, though you will never be able to validate their insights unless you have at least a foundational knowledge of emerging technology.
- Investors also need to understand macro trends: no one should ever ask what the Internet is! If there's a gap here, then investors should seek help. There are lots of technology educators that would love to explain how everything works in dummy terms. But dummy is not recommended here.

CHAPTER 4

Who *Are* These People?

Galloway (2022) sets the table:

"Entrepreneur is a synonym for salesperson, and salesperson is the pedestrian term for storyteller. Pro tip: No startup makes sense. We (entrepreneurs) are all impostors who must deploy a fiction (i.e., story) that captures imaginations and capital."

He goes on:

"This is not the same as lying. There's a real distinction between an entrepreneur and a liar: entrepreneurs believe their story will come true."

"The Valley's 'always tell the truth' sermon is reductionist and hypocritical. It ignores the fact that many of our nation's most valuable companies are priced on promises of technologies that don't exist."

So what do you think? Is Galloway just a grumpy old entrepreneur/professor, or is he on to something? Is his analysis too pessimistic, realistic, or optimistic? Clearly he's not an optimist—or is he? When I read his analysis, I thought it was a pretty accurate description of how the start-up world really works. Is there a path-to-cash that works better than others? Is Galloway just doing us a favor by anchoring us in reality? You bet he is.

The Cast of Characters

It's obviously important for entrepreneurs to understand the players—including themselves. Over the years, I've met all kinds of innovators, entrepreneurs, investors, bankers, lawyers, consultants, and other players in the innovation and entrepreneurialism game. Many are very legitimate players, but many are incompetent, unprofessional, hypocritical, self-delusional, and unethical. (Don't ask me to document the distribution across the legitimate/twisted continuum. Just do it for the players in *your* world.)

Occasionally, they even break the law.

The more you really know about the players, the more successful you'll be, so pay attention.

Entrepreneurs

Let's start with entrepreneurs. There are all kinds of them. Some are just businessmen and businesswomen looking for ways to make a lot of money as quickly as possible. The accolades we pay to so-called *serial entrepreneurs* are misleading, unless serial means *subject matter entrepreneurs (SMEs)*. For example, entrepreneurs who move from industry to industry chasing trends are much less likely to succeed than entrepreneurs who have demonstrated track records in specific industries or technology clusters about which they know a lot. Which are you?

Takeaways?

- Measure the subject matter distance across entrepreneurial experiences. If entrepreneurs move from dentistry to dermatology, they're not serial entrepreneurs—they're *wannapreneurs* or *opportuneurs*, trends chasers looking to cash in on what someone said at a winetasting party was an opportunity to make some quick money.
- On the other hand, if they have a portfolio of similar successful and unsuccessful entrepreneurial experiences, they're *subject matter entrepreneurs* who should be taken more seriously.
- Hopefully, you're an SME and not an opportuneur. But, as discussed, if there are weightlessness opportunities, they should be considered. (I realize this sounds like a contradiction, but I'd never tell an entrepreneur to walk away from an opportunity to make money. Ideally, the walk is not too far from their subject matter expertise.)

Opportuneurs are very different from **entrepreneurs-with-themes**, like digital security, architecture, healthcare, pharmaceuticals, and biotechnology.

Entrepreneurs-with-themes stay in their swim lanes and accumulate more and more domain knowledge along the way. If they're at all introspective, they learn from their domain mistakes, which makes them better entrepreneurs. But moving from failure to failure in search of a jackpot is a red flag to entrepreneurial partners and investors. If an entrepreneur fails in the pharmaceutical domain and then moves to dental office design, it's not clear how anything was learned from prior failures. Worse, it means the opportuneur is always climbing a new learning curve.

Many serial entrepreneurs believe they have generalizable skills and competencies that can be leveraged across multiple vertical and horizontal industries. *"I can sell!"* is one I've heard over and over (and over) again. The assumption is that *selling* is the same across industries. The assumption that sales pitches, tone, subject matter expertise, and attitude are the same across industries is ludicrous, but many serial entrepreneurs try to pitch their abilities across what they spin as generalizable skills and competencies.

Remember

- Be wary of overly glib entrepreneurs who believe that they can sell anything. Or build anything. Or manage anything. They can't. (I hope that's not you.)

There are lots of smooth talkers capable of wooing all kinds of naïve professionals who cannot separate reality from hype. If a fast-talking, glib entrepreneur is surrounded by colleagues who barely say a word, you've encountered an *opportuneur*, someone who understands the value of *venturetainment*. They're often just conmen and conwomen.

There are lots of professionals around the innovation and entre-preneurial process that have very little but personalities, titles, and (sometimes old) relationships in their portfolios.

Notes

- Not all entrepreneurs are credible. Many don't even have the most basic entrepreneurial skills and competencies, but some of them bring other things to the table, like personal connections, name recognition and, therefore, the ability to connect people with money (with firm handshakes and great smiles). Value propositions can be challenging. Do you know how to use people to your advantage, even when their skills, competencies, and experience are uneven or downright bad?

- Don't become frustrated. There are many characters in this movie playing different roles. Some are interesting and some are instantly forgotten. But in a well-directed movie, they can all be exploited. As you develop your entrepreneurial instincts, make sure you learn how to categorize and assess the players—including yourself. *Also learn to suffer fools and frauds well—and quickly.* This skill is necessary in a world with so many fools and frauds.
- There's not much to be gained from complaining endlessly about how ridiculous the questions at a pitch meeting are, how clueless the people in charge are, or how they ascended to positions of power and influence. Entrepreneurs need money, teams, and partners. You seldom find all three in a one place.
- What kind of entrepreneur are you?
  o   What do you know?
  o   Who do you know?
  o   How appropriate is your personality?
  o   What do you know about yourself?
  o   How are you perceived?
  o   What's your *brand*?
  o   Can your morph at a moment's notice?

Go to your LinkedIn page right now. Read it from the perspective of a customer and an investor. What would they take away from your profile? What do **you** take away from your profile? (Ask someone you don't know very well what they think.)

Remember

- Self-awareness is one of the most important skills an entrepreneur can possess.

- If an entrepreneur has no idea what people think about his or her abilities or past performance, then the entrepreneur—perhaps you—will fail.

Another step you should take to define your entrepreneurial abilities and commitment is to *vet yourself and your entrepreneurial idea* with an objective colleague whose relationship you don't value. This process goes by lots of names, but it's intended to vet, pilot, and test run who you are and what you intend to do: *if someone benchmarked you, what would they discover? Seek truth-to-power every time.*

Are you domain light or heavy? Do you know a lot about computer software, digital security, architecture, or cloud delivery models? Are you better at technology management than technology innovation? Are you a founder who's better at marketing than making? Are you a trends chaser?

Some Questions

- Do you have any experience as a real entrepreneur?
- If you're a first-time entrepreneur, you will need to surround yourself with entrepreneurs who have walked the walk and talked the talk. Otherwise, you will likely lose everyone's money —assuming you can raise any.
- Are you stubborn?
- Can you pivot in response to the market and your competition?
- Do you believe you know more than anyone else on your team or what any of the external critics might say about your baby?
- Can you manage your emotions?
- Are you rough or smooth around the edges?
- Can you text, call or email more than 10 investors right now and quickly raise money?
- Are your investors happy with you, or do they feel neglected or even burned?
- Can you attract significant talent?
- Are you a visionary, a fundraiser or an operator?
- How many professionals and investors would travel with you again?

Many entrepreneurs are good visionaries but horrible operators. If you're a bad operator, you will need help. If you're a bad fundraiser, you will need help. If you're a good operator, but a terrible visionary, you will need help.

More Questions

- Do you know what you do well and do poorly?
- Can you speak? Can you engage different kinds of professionals for very short or extended periods of time? Can you listen patiently to the same stories day after day?
- Can you write? Can you develop presentations at a moment's notice, or do you need long lead time to assemble an argument or status report?
- Are familiar with the AI tools that can make your more productive and presentable?

There's one huge exception to the preceding rules. If you find yourself in a white-hot market—like what we experienced in the dot.com era and the current frenzy around GenAI—you will experience some degree of entrepreneurial weightlessness. The normal rules of the road will evaporate and every entrepreneur, opportuneur, and wannapreneur can be funded—at crazy valuations. If you find yourself in such a market, think about how you want to play your hand. While you may be able to raise fast money from dumb and disciplined Angels, or even institutional investors, be careful about terms and personalities. ***But as suggested, you should become weightless.***

Investors

Theranos (Dickler, 2022) is especially instructive. How in the world could so many wicked smart, experienced investors and celebrity board members be fooled so thoroughly by an entrepreneur who almost never blinks?

Nearly a decade ago, Elizabeth Holmes raised $945 million from high-profile investors including the family of former Education

Secretary Betsy DeVos, Rupert Murdoch and the Walton family of Walmart fame.

To lure investors, witnesses testified that Holmes' claims about the company's blood-testing technology were either exaggerated or false. In the end, jurors convicted Holmes of wire fraud and conspiracy to commit wire fraud.

Innovators who seek to revolutionize and disrupt an industry should tell investors the truth about what their technology can do today, not just what they hope it might do someday. Sure, there's always an element of "fake it till you make it," the gap between fake and make cannot be so large that the endgame is impossible to describe. In this case, the gap widened over time as more and more money was fed into the company. You don't want to be a gap manager. You want to tell the truth about where you're going and how you hope to get there, even if you cannot name every road you plan to take.

Who were some of the best and brightest who bought the story? Can you believe George Schultz, Henry Kissinger, William Perry, Rupert Murdoch, Betsy DeVos, Tim Draper, Larry Ellison, ATA Ventures, Partner Fund Management, Fortress Investment Group, Walgreens, Cox Enterprises, AmeriHealth Caritas, Capital BlueCross, James Mattis, Richard Kovacevich, Robert Kraft, Alice Walton, and William Foege, among others? No you can't: they're way too smart to fall for such a story, right? Way too smart to avoid questions about the entrepreneur, the technology, or the business model, right? You know the answer. *"If Henry, Rupert and Betsy invested, it's probably OK."* It's not because all these investors had deep domain expertise, that's for sure.

Lesson?

* Make sure to link your story to reality. In other words, don't drink the deal aid you prepare for everyone else—unless you need to drink it yourself.

You need funding. You may need money right now. Where can you get it? From yourself, friends, family, Angels, crowd funders, VCs, incubators, and grants (like SBIR grants). But remember that you're selling parts of your company whenever you raise money in—according to the US Securities and Exchange Commission 2024—lots of ways:

- Stock
- Membership Interest
- Stock Option
- Restricted Stock
- Convertible Instruments
- Debt

So what do you do?

This is an incredibly important question for all entrepreneurs. Do not explore the answer casually. Do not simply do what you know—or what your entrepreneurial colleagues have done. Or talk to VCs you've met at parties. Pay close attention to all the options you have.

There are various kinds of investments and investors. Let's start with the start-up financing cycle, which identifies the traditional steps in the fundraising process over time. You should already be familiar with this cycle, so I will go fast.

So What's *Seed* Capital (Wikipedia)?

"Seed money, sometimes known as seed funding or seed capital, is a form of securities offering in which an investor invests capital in exchange for an equity stake in the company. The term seed suggests that this is a very early investment, meant to support the business until it can generate cash of its own, or until it is ready for further investments … seed capital can be distinguished from venture capital in that venture capital investments tend to come from institutional investors and tend to involve significantly more money, and arm's length transactions, and much greater complexity in the contracts and corporate structure that accompany the investment. Seed funding involves a higher risk than normal venture capital funding since the investor does not see any existing projects to evaluate for funding."

For seed funding, the popular rule of thumb is to turn to founders (you and your team), then friends, family, and Angels—*but this rule should be violated.*

Remember!

- ***Do not take money from friends or family—ever—unless you're—and they're—prepared for the friendships to die-over-money, which most Angel friendships do.*** While there's lots of discussion in the community about the pros and cons of taking money from friends and family, you should emphasize the cons.
- The goal of seed financing is survival. But note that survival assumes revenue growth (or, in some cases, amazing IP). If growth sputters, you will fail—even if you're able to convince investors to keep writing checks. The financing cycle acknowledges the overarching importance of revenue growth—so pursue revenue relentlessly—even when you are pre-revenue!

Everyone's excited the day the money changes hands. After the euphoria, it's often downhill. ***The time it takes for the marriage to dissolve is directly proportional to the size of the check, IP progress, and revenue growth. Small investor checks keep friend/entrepreneur marriages alive longer than big ones, which almost always end in divorce (because most startups fail).*** Of course, friendly seed capital could generate millions of dollars, but it's far more likely for the seeds to die for lack of revenue than sprout dollars.

Angels

Angel investors are very different from friends, family, or institutional venture capitalists (Wikipedia):

"Angel investors are often retired entrepreneurs or executives, who may be interested in angel investing for reasons that go beyond pure monetary return ... angels typically invest their own funds, unlike venture capitalists who manage the pooled money of others in a professionally-managed fund. Although typically reflecting the investment judgment of an individual, the actual entity that provides the funding may be a trust, business, limited liability company, investment fund, or other vehicle."

By the way, unless you're developing a kick-ass new technology product, forget about crowdfunding. It's usually a waste of time. You will only raise a limited amount of money, and your more serious investors will see crowdfunding as your inability to raise founder, co-founder, Angel, or venture money. Yes, there are some exceptions. A few companies have raised meaningful money, but do you want to start fundraising as an exception?

Professional, disciplined Angels (O'Connell and Curry, 2022) can be good partners primarily because their expectations are preset: they have a *high-risk/high-payoff* perspective. This of course does not mean they expect to lose all their money. You will **always** have to communicate with disciplined Angels continuously, honestly, and consistently. Disciplined Angel investors are often part of more organized Angel investor networks known as *accredited investors*.

There are two kinds of *dumb Angels*. Dumb-Angel-friends (DAFs) write checks because they have a relationship with the entrepreneur and fancy themselves disciplined investors, which they are not. They represent a rich source of funding for well-intentioned entrepreneurs. They're good for delusional entrepreneurs because they can tell the DAFs they will make a lot of money because the entrepreneur is sure there will be a high payoff and because many entrepreneurs believe the hypotheses they offer will be confirmed. (This is also known as the George Constanza Law: *"it's not a lie, if you believe it."*) Avoid DAF money.

The other kind of dumb Angel is unknown to the entrepreneur, but part of a network of investors who like **playing** investors. Sometimes these dumb Angels are lone wolves who hear about deals through their dumb Angel networks or through some other social or professional grapevine.

The problem of course is that it's hard for many entrepreneurs to tell the objective truth. It's hard to tell Angels that there's a much better chance they'll lose most if not all of their money (and will likely be asked for more) than to promise a huge return on their investments. But promise they do—in every way but directly. *Is this lying?* Let's call it optimism. Many entrepreneurs believe every word of their own pitches—or maybe they don't—it's often hard to tell. (Remember what Galloway tells us.)

DAFs are also much more emotional and therefore must be managed more carefully than disciplined Angels. Disciplined, professional Angels understand due diligence. They also understand some investment domains. They will ask the entrepreneur tough questions about the market, the technology, the competition, and the team. If you cannot answer basic questions, you will not get their money. Does this mean that disciplined Angels are looking for sure things, or that they expect no bumps in the road? Not at all. But they want to increase the (already low) probability of a return on their investment.

They will also require transparency, so be prepared to keep your business model and the books open for inspection and discussion.

Takeaways?

- Please, please, please administer investor IQ tests of your Angels. *While stupidity can be appealing, eventually you will pay the price.* So avoid dumb Angels as consistently as you avoid taking money from friends and family.
- The ideal Angel is disciplined, experienced and accredited, especially in your business domain.
- Angels fly around various locations. You can find them on AngelList, the Keiretsu Forum, Gust, the US Angel Investment Network, the Angel Capital Association, and at the Band of Angels. They're everywhere. But, as usual, the best way to find

them is through your relationships, or the relationships in your immediate orbit.

- Managing disciplined and even dumb Angels requires skill, commitment, and transparency. Entrepreneurs must respect their Angel investors—even if the Angels have no idea what the entrepreneur is doing. *Infrequent communication is a huge mistake.* It's also professionally disrespectful.

- Avoid one-on-one communications with your Angels because Angels talk among themselves and will share different messages about the state of the company. Unless messages are perfectly consistent, this is a potential nightmare for entrepreneurs—for you. *So do official, frequent, consistent and documented group updates with you Angels.*

Lessons?

- Proactively solicit questions; encourage discussions about your business model. Your investors are literally your life blood.

- It's important for entrepreneurs to respect their investors and speak with them often, and make certain that these communications are open and consistent. Beware of entrepreneurs who avoid frequent group communications. Some entrepreneurs—I hope not you—prefer a *divide-and-conquer* approach to investor communications. This approach allows entrepreneurs to describe different realities to different investors at different times. But it's only a matter of time until the realities collide.

- If you're the entrepreneur, please keep communications open, consistent, specific, frequent, and scheduled. Remember your investors are your bank, and it's not good business to confuse or anger the bank—especially because you may well need additional money from the same bank.

- *Investor fatigue* is real. One way to avoid it is to keep your Angels happy, and the best way to do that is to keep them informed on a scheduled basis. You must also assume that your Angel investors will communicate among themselves. The last thing you want is Angel distrust or the discovery that Angels are receiving different messages from you or your team. There is no faster path toward Angel investor activism (and sometimes even lawsuits) than investor confusion.

- Never forget about SBIRs. You can end-run all of the Angel issues with "free" money from the government.

I've been down all these paths in my career. Friends and family want to support you because they love you and believe in you, even though they have no idea what you're doing. The biggest Angel mistakes I've made in my career were to convince friends to invest along side of me—Angels who relied 100 percent on *my* experience and *my* judgment, not on their own understanding of the investment opportunity. I regret this advice often. (In several cases, I fixed some broken wings with mea culpa checks.)

A quick story. After trying again and again, I didn't hear from the founders of a venture fund in which I invested *for nearly 15 years!* It just disintegrated, and they never bothered to tell me what happened: the co-founders never communicated about the fund's failure! I finally tracked them down and managed to get a letter stating they lost all my money, though it took over a year to get the letter. One of the partners finally apologized for the *15-year communications gap*. My accountant was the only one who was happy. Don't do things like this. It's unprofessional and unethical.

One of the worst ways to raise money is with personal debt. One of the best ways to raise money is with SBIRs, and if that fails, raise money with simple agreements for future equity (SAFE; Thomson Reuters, 2024):

A SAFE is an investment contract between a startup and an investor that gives the investor the right to receive equity of the company on certain triggering events, such as a … future equity financing (known as a Next Equity Financing or Qualified Financing), usually led by an institutional venture capital (VC) fund … (or) sale of the company.

According to Investopedia (Hayes, 2024):

> Startups use SAFEs to receive funding without determining a valuation or issuing equity immediately. Investors invest in the startup, but rather than getting shares right away, their investment converts into equity only once a predefined triggering event occurs.
>
> Common triggering events, also known as conversion terms, include an equity financing round, an acquisition, or an initial public offering (IPO). Conversions usually happen at a discount or valuation cap as an incentive to invest early.

SAFE investments are relatively safe (but not as safe as SBIRs).

What about self-funding? At face value, it's appealing as hell because you don't have to spend all of your time raising money or managing investors after you've cashed their checks. Sounds good, right? Unless you have money to burn, self-funding is not a good idea. Why not? Because startups that depend on your deep pocket will not develop as objectively as they will when several—or many—pockets are at work. It's also important to remember that when entrepreneurs successfully raise outside money, they're essentially *validated* (even when the investors are far from brilliant). There's also the momentum that outside funding creates. It's extremely valuable to have investors they can name as supportive of their startup. Lastly, self-funding often creates stress in an entrepreneur's personal life, especially when the partners in that life worry about what might happen if the start-up fails.

Venture Capitalists

I've dealt with VCs for a long time, including my short time as one of them. I've lost count of the number of meetings I've had (and emails I've exchanged) with them over the years.

Here's what I've learned: VCs know what they know, and not much else. So what do they know? How to raise and spend other people's money. Remember that VCs have one raison d'être: money.

It's on me for not working closely enough with domain-savvy VCs: most of the VCs I've worked with would fail an undergraduate course on emerging or disruptive technologies, regardless of how amazingly articulate, handsome, rich, self-assured, connected, beautiful, and affable they might be. A long, long time ago, one of the partners at a venture fund asked me what the Internet was. He called me into his office, closed the door, and asked, *"Steve, what's the Internet … how does it work … what does it do?"* I answered the questions and memorialized the exchange in an email to myself (which I've kept all these years), absolutely stunned that a partner of an *technology investment fund* would ask such a question (though it wasn't the last time a venture capitalist would ask me to explain a basic technology).

I'm still amazed that anyone would trust hundreds of millions of dollars to VCs with little or no understanding of how the technology in which they were expected to invest actually worked. But it happens more often than you might think. So, instead of whining about it— as I just did—just assume your VC may or may not understand the technology that drives the business models of the companies in which they invest.

Because lots of VCs come from banking, finance, mergers, accounting, acquisitions, and related industries, they really don't understand much about retail, insurance, manufacturing, or aerospace, among other vertical industries either. The good ones are high-level synthesizers and abstractors. The *knowledge* they acquire seldom extends beyond the information they receive from other people. They live on the margins of understanding and the boundaries of those margins are defined by those in their personal and professional orbits. VCs therefore tend to rely extensively upon what they hear from their associates, interns, analysts, operating partners—and CNBC. Some of these professionals are solid, but they too generally come from the world of finance (broadly defined), not from the technology world. Is this a bias that just *I* have? Am I the *only one* who sees this? You decide how much technology knowledge and experience is necessary to throw millions of pension fund dollars—other people's money—at entrepreneurs.*

Let's summarize

- Many VCs are self-assured because they have money to invest, because they're rich and because entrepreneurs are always asking them for money. They're not self-assured because of their innate intelligence or their technology or vertical industry domain expertise. Does any of this really matter to you? Nope. Just be aware of the depths of their competence and incompetence. *But remember to never offend the bank.*

So what **do** VCs know?

- They know a ton about investor rights and lots of start-up company legal minutia.
- They understand Operating Agreements and Term Sheets.
- They're good at modifying deal terms.
- They know about intellectual property.
- They're good at employment agreements.
- They can read spreadsheets.
- They understand cap tables even when they're drunk or high and can dissect—and challenge—revenue projections in their sleep (usually by discounting them or attaching them to valuation clawbacks).
- They understand—or at least can point to—all kinds of comparables.
- They're valuation impresarios.

Remember that VCs spend other people's money—not their own. (Note that there's usually a contribution from the venture partners to a management company that runs the funds, though not all VC

---

*It's not just me. There's an ongoing discussion about how little VCs know about the technology in which they invest. When you have some time, Google "how well do VCs understand technology?" You'll note that there's a growing expectation that VCs learn more about technology, especially in the age of AI. Listen to this (Zapflow, 2023): "one of the biggest problems Venture Capitalists (VCs) face while investing in tech companies is that they often don't understand the technology well enough to make informed decisions."

partners invest in the management company). The contribution is often 1 percent, which means that 99 percent of the money comes from the main shareholders of the funds—the *limited partners*—such as high net-worth individuals, university endowments, pension funds, companies, banks, and other funds. VCs make money from management fees, from management fees stacked across funds, from management company dividends (for invested partners), and from carried interest (when they sell companies)—which is why most VCs are rich.

- Most of the success that VCs enjoy is due to their relationships—*who* they know, not *what* they know. It's amazing how much VCs rely on the judgments and work of others and their phone banks to do their jobs. Without their networks, analysts, associates, consultants, and relationships, many of them would be incredibly ineffective. Entrepreneurs need to understand all this before engaging VCs to conduct due diligence on their company's technology or digital business model for potential investment purposes. Entrepreneurs should also understand that this influence path can be manipulated once they understand all of the moving parts.
- One of the outcomes of this knowledge gap is that *you must speak two languages*—venture-speak and tech-speak. Don't get into the technology weeds with Managing Partners. Get into the weeds with Associates and Principals if they're leading due diligence efforts (and if they're capable of holding such discussions). Talk venture-speak with MPs, before or after you talk tech-speak with the due diligence people. Then, well, you get the idea.

Who they invest with, the entrepreneurs they back, and the lawyers and investment bankers (IBs) they hire, explain much more about their success—and their desirability as investors—than their technical knowledge, experience, or luck. If you look at the most successful VCs (defined *only* by their internal rates of returns [IRRs]), you will almost always see repeat performers in their portfolios. Smartly, they go to the same wells mostly because it's just easier to work with the same successful (and even unsuccessful) entrepreneurs and ecosystems than to continuously vet new ones. These entrepreneurs comprise the most essential component of venture capital networks and so-called Keiretsus.

When their investments fail, VCs still get huge salaries and management fees, fly private jets, and take elaborate vacations disguised as deal flow expeditions. When their investments are successful, they get huge salaries and management fees, fly private jets, take elaborate vacations disguised as deal flow expeditions, *and* get *carried interest*, a percentage of the profits from their investments. The traditional 80/20 split (after huge salaries and fees, of course) makes a lot of *lucky* VCs very, very rich. By the way, carried interest is only taxed at around 20 percent (Davis, 2015).

VCs get paid extremely well regardless of how well they perform. Some of you might believe that if a fund fails to return meaningful returns to its investors, the partners of that fund will have a hard time raising another fund. But the facts suggest otherwise: they usually get several bites at this sweet apple. Candidly, this all sounds very smart —and beautifully insider-ish—to me. In fact, the VC business model is brilliant—*for VCs*. All you need are friends in high places. (A tall, handsome VC once told me that he had died and gone to heaven.)

So how the hell does this all work? How can failed VCs get more money to invest? Listen to this (Rao, 2023)—which sounds a lot like a dirty little secret to me:

> "20 VCs are said to earn about 95 percent of VC profits. Since the number of VC funds in the U.S. is estimated at about 1,000, this suggests that about 2 percent do very well and 98 percent are average or mediocre—they fail to live up to the lofty reputations of financial genius that VCs have self-promoted. Interestingly, SPAC promoter Chamath Palihapitiya notes that only about 10 percent of VCs make money. The rest are said to be money losers with a lot of their profits being phantom profits that their investors really do not see."

It gets worse (Rao, 2023). The data suggests that VCs need home-runs to succeed—but can't find them; that most successful VCs live in Silicon Valley where massive ecosystems dramatically increase the probably of success; that *VC returns and funding fluctuate with stock market exuberance—that the top 2 percent (of VC funds) seem to have the talent to build unicorns at all times. The others seem to need Wall Street exuberance.*

None of this directly affects the relationship you build with VCs, but it's useful to understand when VCs pitch you on how good they are. Who knows, maybe they're desperate for a winner!

All of that said, if you're an entrepreneur looking for an investment, or an investor looking to make some money, what should you look for in a VC?

- First and foremost, relationships: who does the VC know, and with whom do they invest, work, travel, and win? Look for relationship pedigrees that include major law firms, successful entrepreneurial testimonials, happy institutional investors—*and prospective customers and acquirers.*

- Interview (over [expensive] coffee or drinks) entrepreneurs who have worked with the VCs in the past. Determine their value as partners. Play golf, chess, Pokémon Go, or Fortnight with VCs and everyone you can find in their personal and professional orbits. Let them win.

- Performance: while VCs win whether they succeed or fail, you need to know what the empirical record shows, not lore or hearsay, but actual results, like the IRR of every fund they've raised—the actual returns the investors received. Take no prisoners here: this is the most important VC due diligence you will ever do. Find out a lot about them on PitchBook and learn your way around VentureBeat, CBInsights, and the National Venture Capital Association, among other databases, reporting and commenting on the entrepreneurial business. Call friends and colleagues, especially those who have worked with the VCs you're considering. Inspect VC performance across the sectors where they place their bets. Some firms are much better at biotech than digital technology. Where's your company? *Match the firm's best performance sector with your company's sector.*

- Advocacy: assess the firm's orientation—is it an entrepreneur-friendly firm or a firm that focuses primarily on itself and its investors? There are strengths and weaknesses with each bias, but remember that entrepreneur-friendly firms have better deal flow than firms with partner biases, and you'll have more flexibility with friendly firms than unfriendly ones.

- Knowledge: while few VCs are rocket scientists, they should know enough about themselves to know what they don't know. There's no more deadly combination than arrogance and stupidity. If you see this combination, run. *You do not want their money, even if it's cheap.* They will be impossible partners.

- Professional integrity: it's important to calibrate the integrity and ethics of VC firms. If you're wondering why professional integrity is so low on my rank-ordered list, it's not because professional integrity isn't important, it's just that the other areas are *more* important—which tells you everything you need to know.

- Are VCs a last resort? Again, the best time to seek VC funding is from a position of strength—when the VCs want you—not the other way around. Real partnerships are based on respect. Financial relationships based on mutual respect will leverage what VCs and entrepreneurs bring to the table. It's your job—even when you have no revenue—to convince VCs that you're extremely valuable and if they don't invest in you they'll miss one of the greatest opportunities of the 21st century.

- If you chase VCs for money, they'll give you as little as they can for as much of your company as they can own. If you're financially weak, they will crush the valuation of your company—if they invest at all (and they probably won't). Why? Because they can—and because weakness is red meat to VCs. Always remember why VCs exist—and it's not to make you happy, create jobs, or contribute to the community. No matter how many charity balls they attend, golf outings they organize, how friendly they are, or how many political candidates they back (though they must be very careful here [Alden, 2014]), they're one-celled organisms constantly in search of more and more (and more) money for themselves and their investors—in that order. Today's so-called tech-bros of Silicon Valley are perfect examples.

I have friends who are VCs who are absolutely flattered by this description of their professional lives. They love being greedy sharks. They admit they're only after the money—and don't give a damn who knows it! I also have VC friends who believe the description is wrong, unfair, and just plain mean, and that they're really about job creation and the public good. That said, all of them are pretty rich. (Some irony? Some of the VCs who believe they're job creators are investing in AI companies designed to obliterate as many jobs as they can.)[†]

As you already probably know (Wikipedia):

Venture capital is invested in exchange for an equity stake in the business. The return of the venture capitalist as a shareholder depends on the growth and profitability of the business. This return is generally earned when the venture capitalist 'exits' by selling its shares when the business is sold to another owner.

Because investments are illiquid and require the extended time frame to harvest, venture capitalists are expected to carry out detailed due diligence prior to investment. Venture capitalists also are expected to nurture the companies in which they invest, in order to increase the likelihood of reaching an IPO stage when valuations are favourable.

This need for high returns makes venture funding an expensive capital source for companies, and most suitable for businesses having large up-front capital requirements, which cannot be financed by cheaper alternatives such as debt. That is most commonly the case for intangible assets such as software, and other intellectual property, whose value is unproven. In turn, this

---

[†]Google search "are VCs good people or just sharks?"

explains why venture capital is most prevalent in the life sciences, in biotechnology and, of course, generative AI (GenAI).

VCs provide different kinds of capital:

- (Sometimes) seed funding, though most VC firms are not always the best source of seed capital.
- Early-stage funding, after a company achieves traction.
- Growth funding, after a company penetrates the market it often seeks rounds of funding (Series, A, B, C, and so on).
- Mezzanine funding that supports growth for a company that experiences early, profitable success.
- Bridge funding when a company needs money between rounds of funding.
- Debt financing.

Remember (Wikipedia):

> VCs also take a role in managing entrepreneurial companies at an early stage, thus adding skills as well as capital, thereby differentiating VC from buy out private equity, which typically invests in companies with proven revenue, and thereby potentially realizing much higher rates of returns. Inherent in realizing abnormally high rates of returns is the risk of losing all of one's investment in a given startup company.

There are *A* players and *B/C/D* VC players. *A* players have terrific deal flow and more profitable exits than B, C and D players. Major league entrepreneurs who have been successful look to A players for funding, and VCs look for entrepreneurs who can hit home runs. This is a relatively closed loop.

Who are the players? You need to know who they are by number of deals they do, the size of deals the stages of the deals, and the domains in which they specialize.

The most active venture investors include (TRUiC, 2024):

WHO ARE THESE PEOPLE?   79

- "Sequoia Capital
- Andreessen Horowitz
- Accel
- Kleiner Perkins
- Bessemer Venture Partners
- Intel Capital
- New Enterprise Associates
- Khosla Ventures
- Benchmark
- Canaan Partners
- RRE Ventures
- TCV
- Founders Fund
- Index Ventures
- Mindset Ventures
- GGV Capital
- Menlo Ventures
- Greylock Partners
- IVP
- York IE
- Lightspeed Venture Partners"

B players are just that: *good enough* but by no means exciting to entrepreneurs with A player relationships and track records. C players often lose money. Many of them become zombies (Milburn, 2015). C players are also often copycats, and often bad ones. B players follow the momentum created by A players. They're happy to follow the lead of venture adults with positive IRRs. B and C players like to syndicate with A players—if they're lucky. Some B players pursue side-by-side investments with A players—again, if they're lucky. At Safeguard, for example, lots of entrepreneurs came to us after they had been rejected by A (and even B) players; same for TL Ventures. (How do I know that? They told us.)

VCs chase growth. They move up and down the investment stage as well as the domains as the market dictates. Very few of them create markets from their industry or technology targeted funds. There are some exceptions, of course, but most VCs are *reactive* to trends and trajectories, not *proactive*.

But there's another kind of venture money entrepreneurs should explore: corporate venture capital (CVC) funds—which actually have the same percentage of successful exits as private equity VCs.

So—and this should be obvious:

- Start-up entrepreneurs should look closely at CVCs after they've looked at SBIR programs and disciplined/accredited Angels. But remember that CVCs are generally more interested in technology that will enhance their business models, products, and services than dressing up a company for sale (to feed its IRR). This is an enormously important distinction—especially if a CVC offers better deal terms than a private equity venture capitalist (Arribas, 2022). But they're out there and they will talk with you.

Over time, some VCs move down the financing cycle in response to external market trends, perceived risks, or changes in leadership. During the dot.com boom, VCs were happy to invest in startups and very early-stage companies, but after the dot.com crash and especially after the financial crash of 2008, many VCs moved downstream to more established companies. While they reduced risk, they also reduced hockey stick gains. High-risk/high-reward was replaced by lower-risk/lower-reward. The problem with these swings is that the investment thesis among VCs and other instruments—like index funds—blurs: since 2009, for example, index funds generated higher returns than many downstream private equity venture funds. So why invest in venture? It's all about that illusive unicorn that can change everyone's life.

In the Philadelphia area, seed and early-stage investors include Ben Franklin Technology Partners and First Round Capital, two funds extremely kind to startups. Ben Franklin Technology Partners describes its mission this way:

We stimulate entrepreneurial potential, economic growth and innovation in Southeastern Pennsylvania by providing the

Capital, Counsel and Connections that accelerate the formation and growth of both technology-driven enterprises and partnerships that create sustainable employment opportunities and spur the development, commercialization and adoption of advanced technologies … entrepreneurs gain momentum by working with the leading seed stage capital provider for the region's tech sectors.

First Round describes its mission this way:

"It's never too early to reach out, but it can be too late. We don't see divisions between angel, seed and pre-seed—we're interested across the board and find that founders' needs are the same early on. In fact, most of our 300+ companies came to us when they were a couple people and an idea, having raised no capital before they met us. So even if you don't think you're ready, we'd still like to get to know you. Maybe we can even help in the meantime."

Robin Hood Ventures is a group of experienced Angels in the Philadelphia area who fund startups and early-stage companies[‡]:

"Robin Hood Ventures is a group of Angels: investors who provide financing to early-stage companies in exchange for an equity share of the business. We invest to obtain a favorable return on our money, to participate in the entrepreneurial process, and to catalyze economic growth—in the Philadelphia area, the mid-Atlantic region, and beyond."

Lessons?

- Know your investors and understand their tolerance for risk long before you speak with them. Make sure you match your performance with their investment criteria, and make sure you're aligned with their exit expectations. If not, you might end up in

---

[‡]You might also consider joining them as an investor!

a fight with your principal investor about when and how to sell your company, or when to raise more money. This is a fight you want to avoid.

- Remember, however, that the lower the risk tolerance, the higher the valuation the investor should pay. This is simply because investors should pay for lower risk—which professional investors (and seasoned entrepreneurs) understand all too well. So if your company is downstream and revenue/profit positive, you're expensive.

Economic times define funding opportunities and risks. When there's a boom, everyone wants in. When there's a bust, Vanguard's Index Funds look pretty good (Mulcahy, 2013), which is essentially where downstream venture investors play (on a company-by-company basis versus an index fund)—even if you have to torture them to admit it!

So?

- Where are you, where is your company, and what are your VC options and targets?
- What kind of market are you in? Do you know? Make sure there's a match.
- Listen to recession forecasters because the value of your company will rise and fall with the state of national and global economies. Are you an *A* entrepreneur or a *B* or *C* player? Be honest with yourself, your team, and your investors—and seek players at the same level.

What's the unspoken modus operandi of a venture firm? Are they investors, partners, or jerks? Mulcahy (2013) discussed the *Six Myths About Venture Capital*:

"Myth 1: Venture Capital Is the Primary Source of Start-Up Funding
Myth 2: VCs Take a Big Risk When They Invest in Your Start-Up
Myth 3: Most VCs Offer Great Advice and Mentoring

Myth 4: VCs Generate Spectacular Returns
Myth 5: In VC, Bigger Is Better
Myth 6: VCs Are Innovators"

Lessons?

- Do your homework: first and foremost, determine who you directly or indirectly know. Either contact VCs directly or through warm introductions. Cold calling is a waste of time.
- *A* players' money is more expensive than *B* or *C* players' money. They will take more equity simply because A players can take more equity; B and C players will accept less equity for the same amount of money because they have more limited deal flow—but A players have the best relationships and exits.
- As an entrepreneur, it's not your concern whether the firm funding you makes money for its investors, though everyone's mood will be better if it does. You can use the money and especially the connections to launch your Moonshot, and, who knows, maybe even save the fund!
- It's important to understand the motivations of your venture partners and even their investors. Remember that VCs invest in a portfolio of companies hoping one of them will be the one that makes their fund. You should track your position in the fund that invests in your company. If you're in the *maybe-a-unicorn* category, you're OK. But if you fall into the *probably-a-loser* category, you need to prepare for some time in the desert. Remember also that venture funds have a 10-year life span, with the possibility of a two-year extension. Knowing where your investment falls along that timeline is also important. It's better to be at the beginning of a fund's lifespan than at the end unless you're getting follow-on funding. Most VC funds activities occur in the early years.

Remember the SBIR program I described in Chapter 1? The Small Business Innovation Research Program is still going strong and is an excellent source of capital for startups. Note the program's tagline:

"America's Seed Fund." If you think that *government funding* isn't for you, think again. This program is massive and has funded some of the most successful startups in history. Please investigate this source of funding, where you don't have to worry about Angels, VCs or CVCs.

Imagine *that?*

Lawyers

Chances are you've already had a bad experience with a lawyer who allegedly represented your personal or professional financial interests. Chances are you paid the lawyer regardless of how well or badly the engagement ended, and you walked away unhappy. Sound familiar? Sadly, this is one of several professions that often leaves us, shall we say, "unsatisfied." Of course, there are *good* lawyers out there, but the profession fights a negative image that is in large measure of its own creation.

Start-up/venture attorneys are necessary evils. They're everywhere around the start-up process because the innovation and entrepreneurial world is surrounded by money. Unfortunately, like medical insurance, you need lawyers to survive, because the start-up process is legally complicated and because the players are often litigious.

Legal support is a necessary evil—all well and good. But there are issues with entrepreneurial law (and all law, for that matter). According to Walker (2010), there are at least *"10 Reasons Why Entrepreneurs Hate Lawyers"*:

1. They don't communicate clearly or concisely
2. They don't keep me informed
3. They are constantly over-lawyering
4. They have poor listening skills
5. Because inexperienced lawyers are doing most of the work
6. They spend too much time on insignificant issues
7. They don't genuinely care about me or my matter
8. Their fees are through the roof
9. They are unresponsive

10. They are deal-killers[§]

Lessons?

- *Managing legal counsel is a survival skill.* But you may have had only limited exposure to law firms and venture attorneys—which makes you vulnerable. Seek *warm* advice here—and learn about the legal issues that surround the start-up process. Obviously, this does not mean you should seek a law degree, but it does mean that you familiarize yourself with the basics.
- One approach is to seek second opinions on all things legal. The opinions should involve fees, time, and prioritization as well as alternative legal strategies. Fees make lawyers accountable. *Free advice from your divorce attorney's brother-in-law is irrelevant.*
- Another approach is alternative fee structures beyond hourly fees. There's no reason why fixed-price work cannot be negotiated.
- *You should also develop some metrics for legal performance.* How long, and for how much money, does it take your lawyers to get things done? Who are the most efficient lawyers—and which ones are terrible? Which demeanor is the most compatible with your team and your style, and which ones do you never want to talk to again? Timeliness is a critical metric. If your attorneys are unresponsive when you need them the most, replace them.
- *Because the legal world is so tangled, make sure your lawyers are not directly or indirectly conflicted—which they sometimes are.* If they are, fire them.
- Finally, startups should never pay retainers. They should pay by the drink.

My experience with venture attorneys is mixed. They're all expensive, and the larger the firm, the more expensive they are, largely because of

---

[§]If you Google "why entrepreneurs love their venture attorneys," you might get a slightly different perspective.

the overhead and reputations they carry. Lawyers are also incentivized to generate fees, so they often spend more hours than necessary to perform simple tasks. The worst lawyers—and I have worked with some of them—are only concerned with generating fees for their firms, which translates into larger personal bonuses for them and their partners. Remember also who the attorneys represent. If you're the entrepreneur, your attorney represents only you. But if you're an investor, the company's attorney is not always your friend. You may need your own attorney to, for example, examine the books of a company you funded. In that scenario, your attorney will fight the company's attorney, and after many hours, days, and fees later, you may or may not get to see the books. Always beware of conflicts of interest, which are everywhere, especially in larger firms that have clients distributed across the entire start-up process. If you peel back that onion, you might discover some relationships that should make you nervous. Watch this carefully, especially because most, if not all, firms are all-and-only about fees. I once discovered that the same firm was representing both ends of a transaction for different clients. When I raised the issue with the IB managing the transaction, the banker just shrugged.

Investment Bankers

You will encounter IBs—at several stages of your entrepreneurial journey. You need to know who they are, what they do and how they can help—*or hurt*—you.

Investopedia helps with the basics (Kagan, 2024):

> An investment banker is an individual who works in a financial institution that is in the business primarily of raising capital for companies, governments and other entities, or who works in a large bank's division that is involved with these activities, often called an investment bank. Investment bankers may also provide other services to their clients such as mergers and acquisition advice, or advice on specific transactions, such as a spinoff or reorganization. In smaller organizations that do not have a

specific investment banking arm, corporate finance staff may fulfill the duties of investment bankers.

Caldbeck (2014) suggests you ask your IB at least seven questions:

1. "What is your success rate?
2. Why do you love my company?
3. What's the average time for closing a deal?
4. Does the bank have experience with firms of this size?
5. Can you provide five references?
6. Who are the first five people the bank will approach?
7. What are the firm's average fees?"

My experiences with IBs have also been mixed. They often circled like vultures waiting for companies to die. Or they flew around looking for healthy companies to buy or sell. Along the way, they've proved to be expensive—though most work is on a contingency basis—and not as thorough or responsive as I hoped. Many of them are phone banks where they call the same old prospects every time they land a client to buy or sell. But many of them also do a lot of cold calling, which is not what investors and entrepreneurs should expect. IB networks, like VC networks, explain much of their success.

We hired bankers to sell companies that were failing. We wanted to monetize what was left. Note that the *only* incentive IBs have is money, so they will do whatever it takes to earn their percentage of the transaction, any transaction. This means they will represent and sometimes *misrepresent* the nuances of deal terms—to get the deal done. They will selectively communicate to get the deal done. They will rush the process to get the deal done (and move on to the next one). The bankers we hired to sell distressed companies stalked investors to get them to approve and sign documents approving the sale: they called, emailed, and called them again, *selling* the deals to disgusted shareholders who knew very little about the terms of the deal, such as the size of holdbacks (escrows) or the circumstances around how escrowed funds would be released. In these cases, IBs had relationships with the CEOs who were, shall we say, less than transparent to the investors. It's hard to use the phrase too often: just follow the money—and be careful.

IBs desperate for long-term business opportunities can be accommodating, but others can be arrogant and conniving. We watched them but not closely enough. In some instances, we had in-house professionals who understood what IBs are, but in other instances, we flew blind. The lessons are obvious.⁋

The use of IBs to initiate transactions—like venture funding—should be contextualized. If your company is strong and you're looking to merge or sell, IBs can be essential to the process. They'll try to get you the highest price they can because their fees are tied directly to the price: a perfect alignment of outcomes. But if you're looking to sell a failing company, they're your undertakers. Keep this in mind when you hire one to dispose of your corporate body. (All of this also applies to the lawyers who stalk dying companies. Like IBs, they're looking for as many scraps to eat as they can. They all report to the Chief Undertaker.)

What Are the Guidelines?

- Lawyers and IBs—like Directors & Officers (D&O) insurance—are necessary evils. They have nothing to do with your team's ability to develop CustomGPTs or data lakes. But they require as much attention as your technical team and the products and services you're developing.
- Do not completely abdicate the management of the legal/banking team to your fractional Chief Financial Officer (CFO) or fractional general counsel. *You must educate yourself.* I realize this sounds onerous—because it is. But the alternative is to remain ignorant about issues that if mishandled can cost you money, time, and market competitiveness. For example, what if your intellectual property (IP) attorney is slow, incompetent—or worse?

⁋There are those who love IBs. See McCombie III (2022) for another perspective on the value of IBs.

- Entrepreneurial success depends upon your willingness and ability to entrench yourself in unknown subject matter. There's no simple or quick way around this requirement.
- Again, beware of *good guy* references. I cannot tell you how many times I've worked with professionals who were described as "good guys" who turned out to be bad partners. By all means, accept "good guy" suggestions, but before hiring "good guys" make sure they're professional and competent. Do your own due diligence.
- All of that said, if you must beg an IB to work with you—unless you're fire-selling your company—you're probably misaligned with the outcome you want: you want to optimize a situation, and they want to kill-and-eat as quickly as possible. Bankers want to make money and publicize their wins, so if you cannot make them rich and famous, they will avoid you. So be careful here. Like with VCs, the best time to contact them is from a position of strength. If you're weak and want out, hire an IB to dump your company—and accept the details of the funeral. They might succeed and get you a little money. Or they might fail. *But lower your expectations about transparency and the purity of the process.*

Boards of Directors

I've sat on founding boards, boards after Series A financing from institutional and CVCs, and public company boards. Many of the dot.com boards were thrown together overnight: at one point, I sat on seven boards, which was absurd. Start-up boards are often assembled based on relationships and the size of the Angel investment. The number of board seats is negotiated during investment discussions and included in final term sheets.

Not every board is organized as a perfectly professional, legal entity committed to the letter of its operating agreement (OA) or unwavering dedication to the protection of shareholder rights. Many start-up boards reflect the objectives and personalities of founders: start-up boards are often comprised of the founding CEO, his or her buddies, and an Angel investor or two. Boards mature when the real money arrives (from major disciplined, accredited Angel investors, private equity venture capitalists, or CVCs).

One board assignment is worth discussing. Over the years, Directors came and went. I often learned about issues with other board members from the founder who told me (and I hope others) what Directors said or did. Board members were also recruited and often encouraged to write checks into the company and of course were treated according to the size of the checks. Board meetings were often ad hoc and generally without written, vetted, or prepublished agendas. You don't want to be ad hoc about anything.

My experience with another board—LiquidHub—was more stable, though many of the Directors were not that experienced in the technology business in which the company operated. There were also too many board members for a company of its size. The CEO worked hard to communicate with Directors and only occasionally used indirect communicators to communicate the strategic objectives of the company. But overall, board management was very well done, very professional. You want to manage your board professionally.

I've sat on some public company boards—like C&D Technologies—where my contributions were limited, if measurable at all, primarily due to my lack of domain expertise. These companies made a mistake inviting me onto their boards, and I made a mistake accepting. There were times when I had no idea what the C&D CEO was talking about. I was invited off some of these boards after only a couple of years (for lack of mutual interest and competence). All good. I had no business sitting there anyway.

I've also sat on boards—like Coriell Life Sciences—that were well organized and purposeful, where the CEO knew what he needed from his Directors and recruited and managed them accordingly. The presentation decks were prepublished for the Directors to review. Agendas were tight: board meetings often ended early. *All* board materials were stored in one place. I could get to them anytime I wanted.

The best boards are collaborative and objective. I've had the good fortune to sit on some of these boards in the technology products and services spaces.

I've learned some things from all this sitting, though not all of the lessons are fun or friendly:

- CEOs and lead Angel or institutional investors often don't want objective advice, especially if the advice suggests that major changes should be made to the company's strategy and tactics. While we could debate the merits of stubbornness, many founders and their founding investors are often way too sure of their strategies and therefore unwilling to listen to contrarians. *Remember that those with the most gold make the rules.*

- CEOs are often blind to real competition and market trajectories. The conviction and passion that enabled them to start the company also often prevents them from pivoting. Boards can help here, especially if they're encouraged to speak truth-to-power, though this is relatively rare when money's involved, where speaking truth-to-power might cost the board member some money or even his or her board seat.

- Board *politics can be brutal,* especially when board members have personal relationships with management and the investors (or are investors themselves).

- Many board members are "drive-by Directors," who read company quarterly reports on the way to the board meeting, if they read them at all. You can easily spot the ones who prepare and those that don't: remember the advice about suffering fools well? We've all experienced Directors asking questions about things already answered in the pre-read materials.

- ***Board management is a core competency for entrepreneurs.*** Learn by seeking advice from experienced entrepreneurs and Directors. For example, understand the best practice of transparency.

Many start-up boards meet only four times a year—*which is not frequently enough.* They should meet *at least six times a year.*

Compensation is usually in equity—preferred shares, stock options, and so on—that vest over time, not cash, so board members have no immediate incentive to work that hard. They sometimes have little real experience with the business itself. They're often there because they've invested some money, because they represent an investor, because their professional networks are wide and deep, or because they're friends with the CEO or one of the investors. Some board members are elected solely because of their relationships, which is often a very good reason to invite someone onto a board: startups (and all companies) need warm introductions everywhere, and the best board members can open lots of doors. If a board member has operational experience, he or she can also help the CEO improve operations—so long as the CEO is open to advice. If he or she is a domain pundit, then strategic advice can be leveraged—if the CEO is open to advice. Are you open to advice?

What Else?

- Make sure your company's Operating Agreement (OA) speaks directly and purposely to board responsibilities, board election processes, and board composition. This is standard fare in OAs, but read it carefully. As the founder-entrepreneur, you want some flexibility, but your investors will want protection from worst board practices. Your auto-default should be investor-friendly and board-friendly language and guidelines.
- Do a requirements analysis: what skills and competencies do you need? Recruit and staff accordingly—even within investor constraints (which will be formidable). Use the skills and competencies argument to create investor pressure about who should sit on your Board.
- Keep the number of board members initially to three; expand as necessary and required (when you receive Angel, institutional, or corporate money). Five is obviously more manageable than seven: the larger the board, the more problems. That said, investors are routinely granted board seats in exchange for

investments, but pay special attention to the tiebreaker, the fifth, seventh, or ninth seat, which should be true so-called (but not always) independent Directors. You should not cede control of the tie-breaking board seat to institutional investors, though if you take enough money, you might have to.

- Boards are inherently political: plan for it—but don't fuel it. Humans cannot avoid tension and conflict, especially when vested financial interests clash, like when the founding Directors clash with new Series A Directors. Personalities are extremely important to board management (and politics). While many of us resist *EQ*-based performance calculi, personalities that blend are—obviously—far better than those that clash. Interview proposed investor-Directors. If you find an obvious problem, address it immediately. Existing board members should be invited to interview prospective members.

- Communicate *openly, consistently, simultaneously, and frequently* with your Directors. *Do not divide and conquer.* It will backfire. Provide whatever materials board members request—including, obviously, all financial records. An obvious best practice is to have your fractional CFO and CTO report to the board every quarter (ideally more frequently) on the financial and technology status of the company.

- *Task your Directors!* Ask them to sit on various committees (again, assuming you're large enough) and ask committee chairpersons to help with specific projects, even if the *projects* only consist of making phone calls, sending emails, or texting. *Directors can be a great source of talent as well, which you will need as your company grows.*

- Be organized: schedule board meetings way in advance, and call, as necessary, impromptu board meetings. *Agendas (and all supporting materials) should be shared at least two weeks before board meetings. Open data rooms* for Directors to browse board meeting materials, company documents, and financial statements. There's no reason to ever close these data rooms.[**]

- ***Listen to your board***: good Directors are there to watch and help. Ask them to check your thinking, your organizational structure, your go-to-market strategy, your competitive intelligence, and your team—among other operational and strategic initiatives for which you need objective eyes. Pitch them; practice with them. Many Directors have sat in your seat and therefore have a good understanding of your role, challenges, and opportunities. As always, invite them to speak truth-to-power.

- Pay close attention to your timeline. ***Startups need different skills and levels of engagement than early- or later-stage companies.*** When you transition from one status to another, rethink your board requirements. An infusion of cash will always require you to rethink your board, but you should proactively anticipate board requirements in response to market shifts, competitor pivots, cash burn, and staff challenges, which will occur on a regular basis.

Remember your board has a fiduciary responsibility (a legal one in public companies) to the shareholders—not you, except in your role as a shareholder. *That said, remember that many boards are often—can I say this?—obliged to CEOs who buy their loyalty with cash and stock.* Do you want to "buy" some board members? You can if you like, but you won't get much useful advice from Directors who are bought and paid for. Check this with a trip to Yahoo Finance. Look at how many shares Directors convert and sell: do you think there's a correlation between cash from the sale of stock and loyalty to the CEO? Some Directors make unthinkable amounts of money selling shares granted to them as members of a Board. For example, and according to many sources, Robyn Denholm—the Chairperson of Tesla's Board of Directors—sold almost $50,000,000 of Tesla stock in 2024 and $280,000,000 in 2021 and 2022 (Kolodny, 2024). These are really big numbers.

**Companies like Carta provide excellent data rooms as well as an array of other services.

Advisory Boards

Advisory Boards can be pro forma or specifically tasked with projects. They tend to be PR vehicles intended to raise a company's profile through a network of professionals that might help the company with warm introductions and informal advice. I've sat on lots of these boards, and they generally do very little real work: they tend to be window dressing that demonstrates the CEO and the company can attract an Advisory Board of credible professionals. Sometimes, technology celebrities are invited onto advisory boards (if not the Board of Directors). All of that said, you should leverage Advisory Boards by filling them with big brands, venture celebrities (if possible), pundits, financiers, prominent attorneys, and even an academic or two—all for the purpose of raising the profile of the company. You might even recruit an Advisory Board member or two onto the Board of Directors as your corporate status changes.

The Whole Team

There are lots of players in the start-up process. You need to understand who they are, what they do, and what they really want: understanding motivation always explains behavior, so always follow the money.

- You need to understand *all* the players before you invest your life savings and total psyche into your great idea.
- You need to understand the real start-up process and the players that can help you, the players that will hurt you, and the players you may never even see.
- It's up to you to come to this game prepared.

During my career, there have been excellent teams as well as teams lacking some basic skills and competencies necessary to perform their duties. Technology deals—where technologists are buying technologies with no short-term market monetization plans—are the most straightforward. But when there's an expected specific financial outcome of a funding transaction, all sorts of issues, conflicts, inconsistencies, and biases will define the process and the terms of the deal. I know this should be obvious. But what entrepreneurs and their investors need to appreciate is the distortion index of immediate versus longer-term deals. For example, many of the deals that were done by Safeguard during the dot.com days were clearly rushed, and many of the deals done after the crash were also rushed—for completely different reasons. The first batch was driven by opportunities to cash in; the second to cash out. Both kinds of deals featured poor due diligence.

The best deals (for entrepreneurs and investors) are those that proceed through regular order, where proper due diligence is conducted before a transaction is approved. But anyone who has sat inside a VC firm knows full well, sometimes due diligence is short-circuited for any number of reasons. At Safeguard, deals were sometimes just announced. Obviously, some meetings and conversations had occurred, but the full executive and management teams were not always privy to those discussions. If a deal sounded too good to be true or had an undefined personal dimension to it, regular order was sometimes suspended. The sticklers-for-detail were often frustrated by decision-making processes that sent tens of millions of dollars to a specific company or a group of companies that could easily be described as pets. *Do you want to be a pet?*

Entrepreneurs need to understand how they're being assessed. Is the due diligence process real or staged? Will you have to defend every line on your balance sheet, or will you be waved to the front of the line? While you may think it's flattering to move to the front of the line, remember that some partners love dogs, but others love cats. Pet preferences are subjective, and pet entrepreneurs are sometimes mistreated. *You—mostly—don't want to be a pet—unless you're desperate for food.*

Here's a contrarian view about due diligence. Even if your investors give you a pet pass, prepare to provide all the due diligence materials *you* would need to invest in your company. Make sure they see it all, even as they argue about your pet name.

Yes, that's what I said:

- Even if you're never asked, make sure your investors see everything, warts and all, and don't just show them where the landmines are. Remove them, and then present them to your investors regardless of their size and potential lethality. *This is consistent with the transparency best practice.* If you find yourself happy about the questions the due diligence team *didn't ask*, you've violated the transparency best practice.

CHAPTER 5

The Style and Substance
of Startups

There are lots of moving parts here. Form, content, style, and substance *all* play changing roles in the launch process.

Pitches

I hate to begin this chapter with an emphasis on *form* versus an implied disinterest in **content**, or, said differently, *style* over **substance**, but form **and** style are hugely important, especially to investors generally more impressed with a sweet appetizer than a real meal (until they get to the numbers, when they need to know all about the ingredients). But if you cannot get into the investor's head, there's no chance of a full inspection.

Everyone knows how important the pitch is.

Here's a true story that demonstrates several aspects of the importance of *form over content—and then content over form.*

George Heilmeier, the former director of DARPA, was notoriously tough about form **and** content. In fact, if you pitched George, you better know just about everything there was to know about your subject matter. Remember that we had to pitch ideas at DARPA to get funding. While there was a ton of autonomy given to DARPA program managers and office Directors, some DARPA Directors—like George—insisted upon hearing personally about major and especially highly visible research and development initiatives. Sometimes George got very, very involved.

I was a new program manager at DARPA (before I became the director of the Cybernetics Technology Office) and was funding some research—my own research—on crisis forecasting and management which was an extension of my PhD dissertation. We had developed an early warning and monitoring system that was, under the right circumstances, capable of predicting international crises between nations (Andriole, 1976). I was seeking funding for the next fiscal year to further develop the predictive algorithms and build and test a new prototype.

It was a tiny program by DARPA standards—only $5M—but it was beginning to receive some visibility in the defense and intelligence communities. I had worked on the pitch for several weeks. Fortunately for all of us, George's expectations were codified in something that famously became known as *Heilmeier's Catechism*. The Catechism provided a due diligence framework for those pitching to George: everyone knew what he expected to learn from the pitch.

No exceptions.

The five questions that comprised his catechism were insidious in their simplicity:

1. "What are you trying to do? Articulate your objectives using absolutely no jargon.
2. How is it done today, and what are the limits of current practice?
3. What's new in your approach and why do you think it will be successful?
4. Who cares? If you're successful, what difference will it make? What are the risks and the payoffs?
5. How much will it cost? How long will it take? What are the midterm and final exams to check for success?"

I scheduled two hours for the pitch on the Crisis Management Program. I was 26 years old when the director of DARPA offered me two hours of his time. I received my PhD just two years earlier, but George Heilmeier, a member of the National Inventors Hall of Fame (for his work on liquid crystal displays), the owner of 15 patents, a member of the National Academy of Engineering, the Defense Science Board, and the National Security Agency Advisory Board, among other accomplishments too numerous to mention here, offered me two hours of his time.

There I was a 26-year-old DARPA program manager about to recite the catechism to an engineering legend.

I took the elevator up a few floors in a nondescript building in Rossyln, Virginia. When I walked into George's office, he was sitting behind his desk wearing a hat and a raincoat.

Had I made a mistake?

Did I get the appointment wrong?

What the hell was going on?

Panic struck.

"George," I said, *"I thought we had two hours?"*

I was fumbling with a stack of about 25 *viewgraphs,* also known as transparencies, that were shown on overhead projectors (that few people remember today).

"We did have two hours, Steve, but I just got a call from Bill Perry (who was the Under Secretary of Defense for Research and Engineering at the time, who later became President Bill Clinton's Secretary of Defense), *who needs me at the Pentagon right now."*

"Right now?," I said.

I knew instantly that my question was stupid.

"That's what I said," George said, shaking his head and rolling his eyes at the same time.

"Should I reschedule?"

"No, there's a lot going on at the Pentagon and I'm going to be in and out of the office for a while. Since our budget is about to be submitted I need to make decisions about projects right now. When things calm down, I want to hear all about the research ... I actually have some ideas to discuss with you. I'm very interested in predictive algorithms."

"But I have 25 viewgraphs."

"Then pick one, Steve, just one, and convince me. You have 5 minutes. My staff car is here and Bill is waiting."

I picked one slide from the stack and placed it on the overhead projector on George's conference table. It answered most—though not all—of the questions in the Catechism. It was a pretty slide, a graphic summary that told the story of the whole program in one picture.

Graphics … story … summary … all the right pieces to describe a research and development program worthy of DARPA dollars.

George stared at it for two minutes—which is a really long time when no one's speaking and when there's absolutely no sound in the room. I sat down and crossed my legs, trying to fake relaxation.

After what seemed like prison time, George asked, *"who are your customers?"* (Question #4).

"The intelligence community," I answered, *"and I have commitments to test the prototype in Q1"* (Question #5).

"Go," he said. Style over substance? Form over content? Both.

He got up and left the room but grabbed my right shoulder and nodded as he passed by me.

I still have the $5M viewgraph.

I eventually met with George—*for three hours*—to discuss the Crisis Management Program. Those hours challenged me in ways I have never been challenged before. Raw intelligence is intimidating, and George's personal demeanor was also pretty raw. He suffered fools poorly. But I survived—*and earned continued access to George Heilmeier*. Maybe it was because we were both from Philadelphia. Or maybe it was because the Crisis Management Program was solid. Or maybe, just maybe, George found some value in our discussions, which is what I want to believe.

Or maybe it was just the triumph of form **and** content.

Guidelines

Here's an opening:

> *Thanks for coming. I'm here to pitch an idea I believe will save us (or make us) a lot of money. I will take only 15 minutes of your time. I only have seven slides and a short kick-ass demo. Ask me whatever you like whenever you like. Let's go.*

Form **and** style—not just content and substance—are obviously hugely important to everyone. It's how we win arguments, get promoted, get others promoted, communicate, get funding, and define success (even when we fail). Pitches must be short, pretty, and fun. They must also be impactful and creative. They should have as few slides as possible—if slides—based on your audience analysis—are even appropriate. They tell a story—but not a detailed story, lest the audience get lost in the *story* and not the purpose of the story. There should be pictures and graphics. Some preliminary material should be sent to the audience—but not too much. Assume everyone is busy, so make the pitch short and to the point—which you will describe to the audience at the beginning, in the middle, and after your presentation. Remind the audience why you're there every five minutes.

If you're pitching for project dollars, here are some things you might want to keep in mind.

First and foremost, you must establish purpose:

- Why you're there
- What you want
- Why the pitch matters

You should do an audience analysis. Who are they? What do they like, dislike? You should pre-profile them for their style and substance preferences.

You should list three things you want them to know and remember after the pitch. You should reverse-engineer the form and content of the pitch to those three things. If you insist on five or more things, you will fail to communicate.

You should anticipate questions.

You must prepare for these and related questions:
How Much Money Can We Make (or Save)?

- *What's the likely ROI?*
- *What are the best case/worst case scenarios?*
- *Quantify the win/lose scenarios*

What's the Size of the Market (Market Analysis/Customer Testing)?

- *What's the target problem?*
- *How big and profitable is the target market?*

- *How many competitors are in the market now?*
- *How fast are new competitors entering—and leaving—the market?*
- *How fast are their revenues growing? Or shrinking?*
- *Are there any initial clients/customers we can speak with? Who's already on board?*

What's the New, Big Idea?

- *New technology?*
- *New services?*
- *Hybrid delivery model?*
- *Is there any IP? If so, what's the status of the IP?*
- *What's the irresistible value proposition?*

How Much Money Do You Want—and For What—Specifically?

- *How much money is required?*
- *What's the expected monthly cash burn over the next 12 months?*
- *What's your expected burn rate, revenue, and profitability over the next one to three years? (No one cares about projections five years out)*
- *How do you plan to spend the money? Why?*
- *What's the schedule? What are the milestones?*

How Experienced and Successful is the Team?

- *Who's on the ideation team, the delivery team, the board?*
- *What's their combined entrepreneurial history?*
- *Who are the references very familiar with the founding team's experiences we can contact?*

Wrap your answers in a brisk, flexible, fun, and visual pitch—and then go with the unpredictable flow.

As suggested, there's nothing better than *showing*. Demonstration prototypes can be incredibly effective. But they must be *executive grade*, that is, understandable by those with a lot less domain and solutions expertise than the pitch team—and tailored to the specific audience you're trying to persuade. Demos should last five minutes or less. Make sure you back up live demos with screenshots just in case "live" dies. Better, record the whole demo, just in case.

The pitch itself must be *active*. It cannot consist of 25 dead PowerPoint slides with tons of text and graphics on every slide. Everyone hopes pitches will be brief and to the point, and ideally aligned to the audience's catechism. It should have links to graphics and videos with an embedded use case-based demonstration. A prospective client's/customer's testimonial can be very effective.

Make sure you always dry-run your pitch—as many times as necessary. Find some outsiders to inspect the words and music of your pitch play. Listen to their reviews. Adjust, recognizing there's no such thing as a perfect pitch.

At the end of the day, remember that you (and your investors) want to know how you're going to save or make money. The form and content of your pitch must speak directly to these goals.

Lessons?

- Prepare. Understand the form and content that the audience expects. Ask those who have presented to your audience, and solicit their ideas about what works and what doesn't. Ask the audience directly what they want to hear and how they'd like to hear it. Ask how much time you have. Ask about the *must knows*, and always ask about what infuriates them the most about start-up pitches.
- Ask yourself what the audience wants to take away from the pitch. *Identify what you want the audience to remember tomorrow about what you said.* Work back from the takeaways that will serve you best. That's how the best pitches are constructed.
- Prepare for the unexpected. Be flexible. Make sure that whoever is doing the presentation is smart, articulate, and confident—but never arrogant. (If someone in the audience is wearing a raincoat, just go with it.)
- Do the drill: pick one or two slides.

Not everyone on your team is a good presenter. *In fact, you already know that most of your teammates are bad presenters.* But do the bad presenters know who they are? It's imperative that you select the best presenter on the team to make the most important presentations. In fact, you should always use the best presenter to pitch to anyone and everyone that can help the company. If you don't have a superb presenter on the team, get one. If you're the designated presenter but are horrible, replace yourself. *If you don't know if you're the best or worst presenter, replace yourself.*

Use Cases and Demos

Demonstration prototypes are essential to communicating innovation and selling investors on the uniqueness of your entrepreneurial endeavor. Everyone needs to *see* what you're planning to design, develop, and sell. *They also need to see the technology in a problem-solving context.*

One of the best ways to assess new business models, processes, and technologies is to assess their potential in context, that is, how they could be deployed, and how they could solve classes of problems across multiple vertical industries and even disrupt business models and processes for competitive advantage. Scenarios, simulations, and use cases can help assess and communicate potential. For example, business technologists should explain how an app might help an insurance company reach more customers, how a security tool works for a company's supply chain, or how a social media listening technology can enhance data analytics.

These use cases must be specific and reflect precisely how the technology could be used to solve business problems or invent whole new business models and processes. *"I'll show you what I mean"* is the way to communicate what a new technology might do in the marketplace. Games and simulations can help assess impact before deployment. Supply chains can be animated, simulated, and assessed. *What-if* questions can be hypothesized.

Business/technology teams should use these tools to determine where new business models/processes and technologies might impact their company. You should also develop live demonstrations that clearly indicate how your new company's products and services can be changed, improved, or even disrupted. The demonstrations should be flexible. For example, if a prospective client or investor wants to see how a big unstructured data analytics technology works, he or she should be able to plug their data into a pipe that demonstrates how it works. Flexible demos are convincing. Canned demos beg way too many questions— and undermine trust—but should be available should the live demo fail.

Demos again should be board grade, that is, understandable by Boards of Directors and other executives that comprehend business models/processes and technologies only at the highest level (which is a polite way of saying that they usually barely comprehend technology). Said differently, business models/processes and technologies must be demystified (Andriole, 2023). Jargon and acronyms should be minimized. Examples should be straightforward and easy to understand. Demonstrating, for example, how an electronic payment system could accelerate collection, improve cash flow, and generate interest income can be discussed and effectively communicated through an animated scenario. For many audiences, *demo* is the only language that makes sense. Demos should build upon scenario development, use case analyses, and simulation to demonstrate the power and scalability of the technology for which you're seeking investments.

Prospective clients and investors can better understand the potential of emerging technologies with proactive assistance. Every client or investor will ask a series of questions about any business model or technology it's considering. You should anticipate these questions and proactively answer clients' questions, including especially questions about TCO and ROI—the twins everyone loves.

Failing fast and failing cheap is a favorite executive investment strategy. Who doesn't love the idea of investing very little time and money to learn a lot in a very short period of time? Due diligence is a process that prospective clients and investors should understand and implement whenever a simulation and demo graduate to pilot status. At that point, a series of questions should be asked as metrics are developed to empirically assess the contribution the model, process and technology might make to clients.

Takeaways?

- The pitch itself must be *active*. It cannot consist of dead PowerPoint slides with tons of text and graphics on every slide. By this time, everyone expects pitches to be brief and to the point aligned ideally to the audience's catechism. It should have links to graphics and videos with an embedded use case-based demonstration. A prospective client's testimonial is also effective. (Maybe seven active slides and a demo.)

- Make sure you always dry run your pitch as many times as necessary. Find some outsiders to inspect the words and music of your pitch play. Listen to their reviews. Adjust, as always, recognizing there's no such thing as a perfect pitch.

- At the end of the day, remember that you (and your investors) want to know the following:
  - What—and how big and profitable—is the market you're targeting?
  - What's your big idea? Technology? Services? Hybrid? Is there any IP?
  - How many competitors are in the market now? How fast are new competitors entering the market?
  - How much money is required to launch? What's the expected monthly cash burn over the next 12 months?
  - What's your expected revenue and profitability over the next five years? (This, of course, is a wild-assed guess, a WAG, but necessary to make for the 9AM Investment Committee meeting.) What you should do here is identify the drivers of revenue growth, at least as you understand them at the time of the pitch.
  - Who is the founder(s)? Who's on the management team? What's their entrepreneurial history?
  - Are there any initial clients/customers?

- If you cannot answer these questions, you shouldn't even open your own checkbook, let alone ask someone else for money.

Here's an example of how to win—or lose—that involves some fondling.

After George Heilmeier left DARPA, Bob Fossum became the new director. Bob and I got along really well: in fact, he mentored me in ways that George would probably have described as codling. Bob had a child-like sense of humor. The kind of guy that would laugh for hours about a water balloon exploding on someone's head. We had lunch on a regular basis and became friends. I really liked Bob. Sometimes we decided issues by how many peanuts one could get in the trashcan from across the room. (Bob usually won, which always made me wonder if he practiced at home.)

I remember one year when the fiscal year closed, DARPA found itself with some unspent funds. Bob convened a Shark Tank (where he was the only shark). The DARPA office Directors were invited into the tank to pitch their ideas. It was a winner-take-all event: one idea for millions of dollars.

I learned something important that day. Despite all the preparation and practice, we all lost to Gordon Sigman who ran the Tactical Technology Office. *There were five offices, and we all lost to Gordon.* It was open and shut. As soon as Gordon unveiled his idea, we all knew we had lost (see Figure 5.1).

We knew we lost when Gordon gave Bob a beautiful model of a forward swept wing aircraft that Gordon promised to build if Bob gave him all the money. We all watched as Bob fondled the model and smiled when he saw his name—*Robert R. Fossum*—stenciled on the model as the pilot.

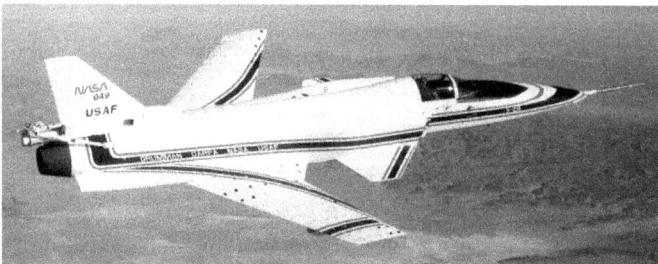

Figure 5.1 Forward swept wing aircraft

Lesson?

- If you can show something, show it (rather than talk about it): there's no more powerful communication than sight, touch, smell, and feel.

Valuation

There's no bigger issue—*or challenge*—for entrepreneurs than the valuation of their company.

Everyone fights about valuation: investors, entrepreneurs, wives, husbands, kids, bankers, lawyers, ex-wives, nerds, ex-husbands—*everyone*.

Part of the reason why there are so many fights about technology and technology-enabled services company valuations is because most companies have some services, some technology, some partners, some clients, and some *vision*. It's the *vision thing* that turns heads—and calculators—but *vision* is arguably gray for lots of companies—and especially investors. Proprietary technology should also turn heads, though here too there are fights. Have the patents been granted? Is the technology truly unique? Is the team any good?

You get the idea.

So, what's your company worth, or, if you're an investor or acquirer, what are you willing to pay?

Entrepreneurs of start-up and early-stage companies need to understand the difference between two opposing valuation methodologies. Whenever they decide to raise money from either Angel or institutional investors, they need to develop pitches that emphasize strategic valuation, not valuations based on rigid or *standard* sales/profits formulae that almost always help investors acquire more equity than they deserve. Operational valuation methodologies are always a trap for entrepreneurs and always a gift to investors.

Operational valuation is the oldest discount trick in the book. If you're a start-up entrepreneur, avoid it at all cost; if you're an investor without much vision—or a so-called *professional investor* with impeccable *discipline*—make operational valuation your best practice.

I remember a discussion I had with a prospective investor in a technology-enabled services company about valuation. He was bullish on the company and fully understood the components: a proprietary technology platform, a portfolio of pending technology patents, a world-class technology development team, a services delivery model, and a basket of client logos even a global consultancy would prize. The company was increasing sales by 50 percent a year, had 75 percent recurring revenue from obviously very happy clients, and was for the first time in its history profitable.

The investor assumed a Yoda-like pose and offered to invest in the company based solely on revenue and profit. *Everything else was discounted.* Put another way, *zero premium* was placed on the proprietary technology platform, the portfolio of pending technology patents or the world-class technology development team. Not much value was assigned to the client logos either, or data around the positive renewal and land-and-expand sales experiences. This methodology yields the lowest possible valuation for an otherwise strong, growing company with proprietary technology and a technology team that would be highly valued, especially in Silicon Valley, where it's not unusual for teams to command a premium of up to $500K per engineer. I argued that assigning zero value to the IP, the technology team and the scalability and extensibility of the technology-enabled services was indefensible. How in the world could these *all* be worthless? He held firm. So did I.

What's happening here?

The greed game played from both sides. Why not devalue as much as possible, invest as little as possible, and acquire as much equity as possible, *or why not ignore sales and profitability altogether and focus on the big, game-changing picture and the proprietary IP?* It depends on where you sit, doesn't it?

Investor-Speak

"So, let's see, Mr. Entrepreneur, your revenue was $5M last year and you were barely profitable, so we'll give you 3X on your booked revenue discounted for lousy EBITDA … or a valuation of $12M." "But what about our technology?," Mr. Entrepreneur says. "That comes with the

deal," the investor says, *"you want me to pay for the forks I use at a restaurant?"* *"But what about the projected revenue of $9M for this year?,"* Mr. Entrepreneur says. *"It's projected, not in the door,"* the investor snaps: *"$12M ... take it or leave it, or we'll talk about valuation clawback!"*

Entrepreneur-Speak

"Let's look at the big picture, OK? Let's project how much of an exploding market—some of which we haven't even defined yet—we can control with this technology and the services we'll build around it." *"What's the size of the potential market?,"* the investor says. *"Size of the market?,"* the entrepreneur laughs, *"what 'market' ... it's untapped and endless!"* *"And don't forget the IP and the engineers who created it—who are still creating more and more IP!"*

The professional investor, who has little market or technology vision, just shrugs. Strategic valuation methodology triggers due diligence processes where the technology and the technology-enabled services delivery model—*and their potential*—are assessed from every angle. Operational due diligence processes include customer calls: *"do you like what the company does for you? Would you buy more of their services? Would you recommend them to a friend?"* It also requires a proctoscopy that examines all expenses, revenue, competitors, and markets over time and into the future, *discounting everything along the way.*

The other (dark) side of the operational valuation methodology is the wide and wonderful *comparables* equation designed to devalue every company on the planet. Why? Because it's always possible to argue that, *"well, you're just like Company A, B, and C* (based on another operational valuation that's been *'set'* by some investors who created the *'precedents')* *and they're only worth X!"* *"Yes,"* the entrepreneur says, *"but Company A is completely different from us!"* *"Not really,"* the investor says, *"in fact, you're the same, and they missed their numbers last year."*

The most important aspect of the valuation dance is the source of the cash. Angels write personal checks. Disciplined, accredited Angels understand risk and dream of strategic valuation-based exits. VCs spend other people's money who generally have no idea how their money's being spent. While repeatedly playing the operational valuation card,

VCs are relatively comfortable protecting—or losing—other people's money. Obviously, they want to make money for their limited partners because that's how they make money for themselves (and generate the next investment fund), but there's always another deal down the road. So even though they're wired to operational valuation, they're also often smart enough to understand the linkage between the two valuation methodologies and how to slice companies into several pieces, or just walk away because *strategic* investments are sometimes just too expensive. As discussed, there's a correlation between what's happening in the venture world today and the popularity of operational valuation. As more and more venture investors move further and further downstream to later-stage investment opportunities, the frequency of strategic valuation has declined proportionately, leaving start-up and early-stage entrepreneurs to fight for strategic valuation with fewer and fewer investors. Some years ago, entrepreneurs had an easier time starting valuation discussions based on the strategic impact their technologies and companies might have on the market. It's much harder now—*unless you're an AI start-up!*

Another class of investor are the companies that often buy and sell companies for operational and strategic value. Facebook paid $2B for Oculus. Microsoft has $10B in OpenAI. These investments are obviously strategic, not operational. Technology companies buy IP and technology teams all the time, even if the revenue model around these assets is unclear. Services companies buy other services companies all the time for as little as they can. Clearly, this is operational. Many technology companies, especially those at the bottom of the food chain (like infrastructure technology providers), have no leverage in these transactions because their value has already been set by some relevant/irrelevant precedents. They're literally trapped in their valuation category and there's no way they can ever escape. Maybe 3X revenue; maybe not. It's all up for discussion.

So given the nuances of each valuation methodology and each class of entrepreneur and investor, let's build a funding strategy that optimizes/minimizes valuation for each class.

Seed and very early-stage companies have no operational value because they have little or no revenue—which is *good* news. There's only strategic value so the fight will be about how strategic your company can be.

Remember

- If they cannot self-fund, entrepreneurs should start with disciplined Angels (after they've explored SBIR funding). Disciplined/accredited Angels understand risk. They're much more likely to endorse a strategic valuation methodology, though they also understand the tradeoff between early risk and strategic valuation and therefore, because they're literally seeding the startup, deserve a good valuation, however strategic it might be.
- Entrepreneurs should never forget how to monetize their strategic importance: even when revenue and profits are exploding, they should never undersell their strategic value. They should link to strategic technology trends and new market opportunities—with AI.
- Institutional funding should only be sought from positions of strength; the same strategy applies to relationships with investment bankers.

VCs are valuation crushers. They will invariably try to apply the operational valuation methodology, no matter what the company really does. They do so because if you show up at a VC's office, you probably need money, and the first desperation test entrepreneurs are given is their willingness to accept a low valuation. VCs administer this test because it protects the investment of their limited partners and, most importantly, themselves.

Corporate M&A teams are both strategic and operational valuation specialists. They understand strategic vision and operational effectiveness. Depending on the vertical industry, some value one more than the other. For example, technology and pharmaceutical acquisitions are often driven by strategic valuation models, where retail and low-end technology services acquisitions are often based on operational metrics.

Entrepreneurs should always profile their investors and acquirers before talking with them. Do they make mistakes? Did Takeda pay too much —*$62B*—for Shire?

The Protocols Are Clear

- Entrepreneurs optimize strategic valuation.
- VCs crush strategic valuation and discount operational valuation.
- Corporate M&A teams are more likely to assess the strategic and operational value of potential acquisition targets.

Investment Term Sheets

The term sheet defines your relationship with your investors. Term sheets are incredibly important. You will need legal help to decipher the term sheet you receive from VCs or other investors. What are they (MaRS, 2024)?

> The term sheet is the document that outlines the terms by which an investor (angel or venture capital investor) will make a financial investment in your company. Term sheets tend to consist of three sections: funding, corporate governance and liquidation.

There are opportunities and risks embedded in term sheets, so be careful. The ideal term sheet, of course, aligns the vested interests of entrepreneurs and their investors. But there's always some fine print that requires careful analysis and negotiation.

Equity terms sheets define the terms around valuation, corporate governance and liquidation. There are standard parts of a term sheet—as suggested by SHAREWORKS (2023):

- "Term sheet negotiation
- Economics
- Valuation and ownership

- Option pool
- Liquidation preference
- Participation rights
- Dividends
- Antidilution
- Board of Directors
- Ownership percentage of share classes
- Investor rights."

Valuation lies at the core of term sheets presented by investors because it defines the percentage of equity the investors will own after an investment is made. There's always a fight about *pre-money* valuation—what your company is worth right now before an investment is made. Do you know? Have you developed a model that defends a specific valuation? Have you looked at comparable companies and their valuation metrics? (*Post-money* valuation defines valuation after the money has been invested in your company.) As discussed throughout, valuation is ideally pegged to your—the entrepreneur's—*strategic* value proposition—how the company is likely to perform in the future versus an operational valuation based on how the company has performed to date, which, by definition, is obviously weak. Performance is almost always defined around revenue. If revenue has been strong, then operational valuation is easy, but if revenue has been uneven or worse, then operational valuation will suffer. If there's an enormous pipeline of revenue in a growing market space—like artificial intelligence—then strategic valuation is possible—and obviously desirable for the entrepreneur.

When there's a legitimate argument about operational versus strategic valuation, valuation ranges—based on actual and projected revenue—are sometimes proposed by investors. This means that if revenue equals X, valuation equals Y. This provides downside protection to investors: if a company fails to achieve its revenue projections, then the valuation of the company falls. But what if a company blows past its own revenue projections? While investors tend to favor downside protection, they're not as happy with upside protection that could result in valuation exceeding the proposed deal terms (surprise, surprise).

Argue your case! If, for example, premoney valuation is proposed at $10M, but adjusted down to, say, $7M if revenue projections are missed, why not propose a ceiling if revenue projections are exceeded to, say, $13M? This provides downside protection to the investor *and* upside protection to the entrepreneur. While it will be a tough sell, you can use the proposal to eliminate or perhaps adjust the floor the investor proposes and set the valuation singularly without reference to revenue.

In a recent term sheet negotiation, the investor—a seasoned VC— offered us a $30M premoney valuation, but it came with a twist. He wanted a $20M floor based on missed revenue targets. That meant if the company missed its revenue, the valuation would shrink by a third, and the $10M proposed investment would—if revenue targets were missed —translate into 50 percent ownership of the company (down from 33% if revenue targets were met)! After we said *no* to the initial valuation proposal, we suggested a $25M to $35M valuation range based on performance. The $25M floor (if we missed revenue targets) and the $35M ceiling (if we exceeded revenue targets) would translate into an ownership range of 30 percent to 40 percent, depending on where the revenue landed, not 50 percent with no upside reward for overperform-ance. By raising the floor and defining a ceiling, we provided downside and upside protection to both parties, but no onerous downside or overly generous upside protection for either. We agreed to split the difference, which is often standard practice—assuming both parties really want the deal to happen.

Remember, valuation is a negotiation. A professional touch— *not a sledgehammer*—is required. You're negotiating with a potential long-term partner. You're also negotiating as a member of the entrepre-neurial society where reputations are built—or destroyed—based on the behavior you display. Negotiate with a long-term outcome—and your reputation—in mind.

Also pay very special attention to the stock option pool the investor defines. Pre-money option pools are often questioned by investors. Why is it so large? Or small? Everyone has a vested interest in the existence of an option pool to attract and reward employees. But the size and terms of the pool are always negotiated in the term sheet. Try to keep the option pool as is and prevent attempts to revalue the option pool *after* the transaction occurs, which will devalue the stock of the founders and early investors.

Term sheets also define *liquidation preferences*—which is downside protection for the investors. Obviously, everyone hopes the company will do well and there's tons of money falling from the sky to distribute, but if there's not, investors want to make sure they're in front of the line whenever money is handed out. This is where the pretty standard *1X liquidation preference* kicks in, which simply means that the investors will get their money back before anyone else (like common shareholders) receives a dime.

Watch out for *participation rights*, where the investors get the right to not only get their money back (the standard 1X liquidation preference) but also get to *participate* again in what's left after the initial distribution of funds. This is an attempt to double dip into the cash that's left after the first dip returns the initial capital investment: not good for entrepreneurs and common shareholders. You might want to fight against participation rights for these reasons as well (FasterCapital 2024):

> "Participation rights can lower the valuation and increase the dilution of the startup. They can also reduce the autonomy and ownership of the founders and the employees. Participation rights can also discourage new investors and acquirers from investing or buying the startup."

Should you—or any investors—expect *anti-dilution* protection? It's a reasonable request by seed-stage investors who buy preferred shares of your company. But realistically, it's protection against disaster—like when you must raise money at a valuation lower than the previous round (the dreaded *down round*). The only anti-dilution protection you should give is a weighted average one, where investors are required to invest additional capital in the event of a down round to earn the protection.

After valuation, control is the most important feature of a term sheet, and control lies in the Board of Directors and the investors they represent. Control of the board should correlate perfectly with ownership percentages, which is another reason why you must negotiate valuation as aggressively as possible. If investors own a third of your company, then the investor is entitled to one of three board seats. That said, nearly all corporate operating agreements (OAs) require an *independent* director, though *independence* is a relative term! While minority shareholders have a vote in the selection and approval of the independent board member, as minority shareholders—and likely new investors—they will generally not try to control the independent board member approval process. They will of course vet candidates, but, by and large the founders will manage the process. But when a larger investment is made, and everyone is aligned with a growth strategy, board control will usually be expanded to include founders, investors, and independent Directors.

Follow the money. If you accept $10M against a pre-money valuation of $40M, you need not share control of the company equally. But if you accept an investment of $20M on the same premoney valuation, you will share control of the company, even though the post-money valuation still gives you control. In that scenario, you and your principal investor would constitute a five-person board, where you have two seats, your investor has two, and there's a near-pure independent director—who only exists in entrepreneurial heaven. Or a seven-person board with the same distribution of seats: 3/3/1. Remember, the larger the board the greater number of problems, simply because humans breed problems. Remember also that investments equal the ownership of categories of stock, such as preferred, common and special. This is important because not all decisions are made by the Board of Directors. Some are made by shareholder vote.

I recently received an unpleasant call from a disgruntled co-investor who asked about how the investors might remove someone from the Board of Directors of our company. I responded that the mathematics simply would not permit it, because when we added up all the voting shares, there weren't enough to accomplish his goal. He was angry and frustrated but understood why bad board members can persist at the pleasure of the founders or the investors for as long as it pleases those in control. I suggested that the mistake was made in the OA and in the terms of the investments made over the years, which leads us to *investor rights*.

Investor rights is a quagmire. No one thinks about nailing down each other's rights when someone is dangling a shiny check with seven zeros. But that's the only time investors and entrepreneurs may get the chance to have the discussion about what happens when things go wrong. Investors *and* entrepreneurs should expect bidirectional transparency, especially regarding debt, stock pools, benefits, or changes to the OA. But there are other areas where there might be considerable debate, such as access to the company's books, inspection of the company's IP, the right to external reviews, and input around the selection of IBs and other professionals. Many of these *rights* are difficult to discuss out of the context of specific scenarios. But there are obviously many that require, for example, full inspection rights. As an entrepreneur, do you want your investors to be able to see everything you and the Board of Directors have done over the years? If not, why not? **My advice to you is allow your investors to see whatever they want to see**, simply because if you refuse them access, you're de facto guilty of hiding something, and why would you deliberately paint yourself into a corner of guilt? It makes no ethical, moral, or professional sense because you will forever display a tattoo on your forehead that repeats **"I never wanted my investors to see what I did with their money."** Or worse, **"I told them that if they wanted to see the books, they had to hire a lawyer."** You never want to hear yourself saying these words.

Operating Agreements

What you can (and cannot do) is defined in your company's OA. But OAs are two-way streets: they also define what investors can and cannot do. Because you are sometimes both an investor and an entrepreneur, the OA will define your swim lanes.

Gemini helps with the basics:

"An 'operating agreement' for a startup is a legal document that outlines the rights, responsibilities, and ownership percentages of each founder within a company, detailing how the business will be managed, including decision-making processes, profit distribution, and dispute resolution mechanisms, essentially serving as a blueprint for internal governance to prevent conflicts among co-founders."

As suggested, OAs play different roles. At the very least, they're two-way protections. They define the way things operate and become the reference document of record—and dispute. Without an OA, everyone's at risk, though most U.S. states will default to the state's OA if no OA has been approved by the entrepreneur and the Board of Directors. The issue of *inspection rights*—like the *investor rights* in a term sheet—is one of the most important aspects of an OA. You and your investors should share transparency as a mutual goal. But many of the disputes among members of a limited liability corporation (LLC) are often about inspection rights.

Here's a legal perspective on what these rights should include (Piercy, 2010):

"Business records (which) can be divided into … three categories:

1. Organizational records (which include) … by-laws, articles of incorporation or organization, operating agreements, shareholder agreements, and partnership agreements … and … meeting minutes, resolutions, and any amendments to operating agreements or by-laws.
2. Transactional records (which) are those which relate to the entity's business activities and relationships with third parties.
3. Financial and accounting records (which) are those which reflect the financial affairs of the entity, including tax returns, balance sheets, profit and loss statements, bank statements, and other documents demonstrating the financial condition of the business."

It's hard to imagine more clarity, right? Remember that regardless of how specific the OA is, there may be challenges. This is where larger issues of integrity and professionalism drive the dispute process. If an investor wants to see the books or inspect board meeting minutes, and the entrepreneur—*I hope never you*—tells them they cannot inspect the books or review board minutes, what's the message? Clearly, if an entrepreneur refuses to grant access to corporate records, there's a larger problem that can be summarized in a single, simple question: *"what are you hiding?" There's no argument an entrepreneur can make that justifies hiding the books from investors—unless there's something the entrepreneur wants to hide*. Asked a little differently, why would an entrepreneur—*why would you*—hide **anything** from investors?

Here's what a typical OA covers. You will need legal help here, so don't offer—or accept—an OA that isn't consistent with state regulations and laws, or mutually agreeable to entrepreneurs and investors. I learned the hard way to have an attorney review OAs before I wrote some checks. My bad.

Typical Operating Agreement

- *Description of the Company* (Formation, Names, Purpose, Office, Registered Agent, Term, Names, and Addresses of Members)
- *Capital Contributions* (Initial Contributions, Additional Contributions)
- *Allocation of Profits and Losses*
- *Indemnification*
- *Powers and Duties of Managers* (Management of the Company, Decisions by Members, Member Withdrawal)
- *Salaries, Reimbursement, and Payment of Expenses* (Organization Expenses, Salary, Legal, and Accounting Services)
- *Books of Accounting, Accounting Reports, Tax Returns* (Method of Accounting, Fiscal Year, Taxable Year, Capital Accounts, Banking)
- *Transfer of Membership Interest* (Sale or Encumbrance Prohibited, Right of First Refusal, Substituted Parties, Death, Incompetency, or Bankruptcy of Member, Death Buy Out)
- *Dissolution of the Company*

- *General Provisions* (Amendments, Governing Law, Entire Agreement and Modification, Attorney Fees, Further Effect, Severability, Captions, Notices)
- Members and Signatures
- List of Capital Contributions
- List of Valuation of Members Interest

Buzz

Innovation, entrepreneurialism, and commercialization all need buzz. Entrepreneurs needs buzz. Startups need buzz. If no one's ever heard about how awesome you are, no one will ever know just how awesome your company is. But if we've learned anything from politicians, you can use social media to manipulate reality and perception.

Just as there's a global media starving for news, there's a business technology media only too happy to tell your story—especially if you juice it yourself with the DIY platforms. Many of the celebrity platforms are closed. Challenge this assertion by calling the editor of *Wired Magazine*, *Fast Company*, the *Silicon Valley Times*, *entrepreneur.com*, and other media that focuses on innovation, entrepreneurialism, business technology, or consumer technology and ask them if they're willing to write a story about your next great thing and the new company you're hatching. You need penetration—which is only achieved through a network of media-ites you must befriend. Here's where your team, your investors and your personal and professional network can help, but your buzz plan must not be haphazard or simply opportunistic: *"just make the call!" is not a strategy.*

Differentiation is especially important. Always be prepared to answer the question: *"how are you different?"* Launching is also important, especially given the reach of social media.

Here's an example of some early buzz from Coriell Life Sciences (CLS), an early-stage company in the pharmacogenomics space.[*]

Here's the initial description of the business and the key messages (the bold is mine):

---

[*]I was on the Coriell Board of Directors from 2015 to 2025.

"Coriell Life Sciences will provide **comprehensive clinical reports** to physicians that will interpret the genetic sequences of their patients indicating their genetically-determined response to certain medications … **with a single test, the 'GeneDose' report will list dozens of the most widely-prescribed medicines available today along with genetic estimates of their effectiveness,** with specific dosing recommendations intended to maximize their therapeutic effects, while reducing the likelihood of an adverse reaction, or interaction with another drug … patients who are sequenced will be able to reuse the results of that test for life."

The company's market space was presented like this:

"**The total U.S. market for Personalized Medicine was estimated at \$232** billion and projected to grow at an annual rate of 11 percent according to a 2009 study from PriceWaterhouseCoopers. The rapid decline in the cost of full genome sequencing, coupled with the significant published research on the use of genetic information in clinical care has created a near perfect environment in which to launch Coriell Life Sciences."

"**The Company's Flagship product will be the delivery of a comprehensive report showing the specific effects of drugs on an individual patient.** Advances in scientific research have now made it possible to show how well a drug will or will not work, or be safe or not safe, for a specific person depending on the genes they carry."

"**Consumers expect physicians to know everything about the drugs they are prescribed.** While physicians are extraordinarily familiar with prescribed medications these same physicians cannot know or be expected to understand the drug:gene interaction a patient might experience when a medication is consumed … **the technology will help a doctor know if the prescribed drug works, how fast it will work, offer some**

suggestions on dosing based on the genetic make-up of the patient, and even suggest whether or not a patient may have a toxic reaction—all based on the intimate knowledge of the patient's genetics."

"Consider for a moment the number of hospitalizations that can be avoided when patients no longer get sick or become gravely ill from their prescribed drugs."

The initial plan changed over time. New partnerships were formed with companies such as ThermoFisher, and new products were developed for the mass market. But if you just look at the preceding **bold italics**, you see a powerful message mostly because it describes effectiveness and cost.

I joined the Board of Directors in 2015 and was fortunate enough to participate in the growth of the company. It would be hard to find a more compelling space than personalized medicine enabled by genomics. This was an emerging macro technology trend we've been tracking for years. When gene sequencing costs fell dramatically, all kinds of business models emerged.

A bed of roses?

Not even close.

We learned that the sales cycle was slow—very slow. We learned that there was at least as much interest in the services outside the United States as inside. We learned that U.S. insurance companies were initially uninterested in the service. We learned that the original revenue model was weak. Should I go on? We learned from the mistakes and adapted as quickly as we could. After we almost sold the company to several companies, we were lucky when one acquired the company's assets in 2025.

The point?

- Pay (early and often) for buzz: dedicate significant resources to marketing and PR, but start and stay with buzz that fuels more formal marketing.
- Creatively engineer buzz informed by empirical market research *and* anecdotes about what might sell.
- Remember that buzz today (and forever) is more digital than traditional, so exploit all the digital channels.
- ***Make sure you explore how ML and GenAI can create buzz.***
- Also make sure that all platforms are used to describe your company. It's no longer just Facebook, Instagram, LinkedIn, X, and TikTok. You need to understand the role that podcasts and livestreaming services like Twitch can play in your buzz campaign.
- Remember, ***you're always the company you keep***. Startups need a combination of professionals who are broad and deep. Some will know a lot about PR, technology, or finance, and some will know a little about everything. The latter are your glue; the former are your arms and legs. Understand the difference.

CHAPTER 6

Skillsets

Here's the list of skills that will serve you well. Study it closely, and take a hard look at your team. Is your team entrepreneurially ready? There are at least two dozen technologies, best practices, and soft skills necessary to optimize innovation and entrepreneurialism. If you want to succeed, you'll need them all. Look carefully at the list of technologies, best practices and soft skills.

Technologies

As suggested in Chapter 3, the technologies you should understand and track appear in Figure 6.1. This is a long list that frequently changes. But the technologies on the list are the source of countless start-up opportunities.

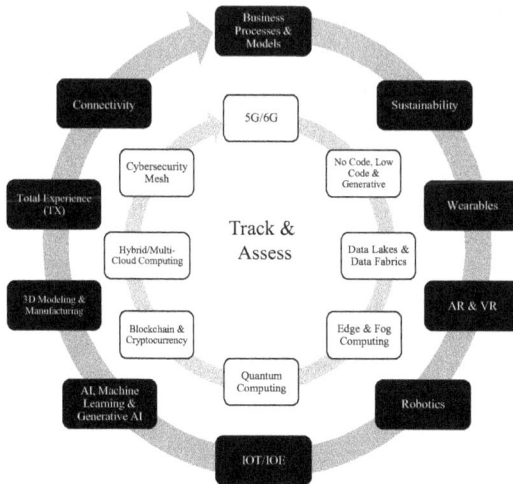

Figure 6.1 The technologies you should track

Infrastructure and applications technologies entrepreneurs should track.

Project and Program Management

The focus here is on knowledge of, and experience with, project and program management tools, techniques, and best practices. It assumes knowledge of, and experience with, project and program management of small- and large-scale technology projects and familiarity with the array of tools available to professional project and program managers. This assumes the ability to manage projects and programs cost-effectively and within task-defined timelines. Project and program managers should be professionally certified (by organizations like the Project Management Institute [PMI]). Your team must understand the importance of project and program management—even as they cope with the chaos of a start-up!

Vendor Management

The focus here is on knowledge of, and experience with, technology vendor management best practices. This assumes knowledge of, and experience with, the development of requests for information (RFIs), requests for proposals (RFPs), and requests for quotes (RFQs), including automated tools to develop and compare these documents. This also assumes the development of detailed service-level agreements (SLAs) and the management tools for measuring SLA compliance. Communications and negotiation skills are also part of this management area. Finally, it's essential to demonstrate knowledge of, and experience with, RFI/RFQ/RFP/SLA-based cloud vendor management, because so much entrepreneurial activity will be defined around the cloud.

Digital Security Management

The focus here is on knowledge of, and experience with, security challenges and processes, including security policies and the adoption of best practices, compliance with industry standards (such as ISO27002), regulatory compliance across the entire university, vulnerability assessment/ remediation, penetration testing, incident response, network and systems monitoring, forensic analysis, security awareness and training, backup and recovery, among others. The focus should be on audit-approved security-as-a-service: even start-ups and early-stage companies must manage security every day.

Business Process Modeling and Mining

The focus here is on knowledge of, and experience with, business process modeling (BPM), requirements identification, modeling and validation, and digital transformation. It also assumes the ability to model existing and future business processes and whole new business models, ideally within BPM and buisness process mining toolsets. This area also assumes knowledge of, and experience with, requirements matching with external vendor capabilities and specific transformation programs and projects. Entrepreneurs must exploit business analysis tools and techniques to evolve their products and services, as well as improve their internal processes.

Metrics and Performance Management

The focus here is on knowledge of, and experience with, operational, delivery, organization and financial metrics, including metrics around online cloud application performance, cloud application availability, delivery incidents, SLA adherence, project performance (especially satisfaction), personnel performance reviews, budgeting and resource costs. Knowledge and experience here also refer to the tools available to track, measure, and report technology performance metrics. Entrepreneurs must track and measure all aspects of their internal and external processes, especially those that touch product development and customer acquisition.

Competitor Analysis

There are few—if any—more important start-up activities than competitor analysis. ***Competitive benchmarking is a core competency***. Entrepreneurs must about know about all competitors. This knowledge is not just cursory: *it's wide and deep*. A simple test is your ability to respond to questions from customers, investors, and bankers about your competitive space. If you can answer quickly and thoroughly, you will pass the test. If you cannot, you will fail.

Accounting and Financing

You must know how to count and how to manage money. Your team must be experienced. You must understand the stages and roles of alternative financing. You must be able to develop credible revenue, expense, and valuation models. If you cannot do all these things, then you must find professionals who can. If you cannot find professionals who can manage your books and your many budgeting and financing processes, you will fail.

Sales and Marketing

Beyond buzz, formal sales and marketing are essential to your survival. These are the skillsets where you need deep experience: there's no faking sales and marketing. You must find and incentivize productive sales and marketing professionals. If they fail to generate the right brand, positioning, and revenue, they should be quickly fired, because failure here is lethal. Sales and marketing professionals must be almost thoroughly digital because sales and marketing are increasingly digital. Professionals here should also understand how to optimize use cases and demos. They should be agile and always aware of the competitive space in which the company lives. But remember that sales and marketing professionals fail a lot, so lower your expectations about their performance and be prepared to change them out frequently.

Legal and Investment Banking

Most entrepreneurs fail to appreciate the best, worst, and emerging best practices around entrepreneurial legal processes and the processes around engagements with investment bankers. First-time entrepreneurs will likely know virtually nothing about these processes. It's imperative that you and your team develop, acquire, or outsource the skillsets necessary to manage and optimize legal and investment banking relationships. Founders need to understand the basics here.

There are also necessary soft skillsets.

Written Communications Skills

The focus here is on experience writing reports and creating presentations that are easily understood and therefore actionable. *The key to communication is purposeful brevity*: is the team capable of such (written) communication? Written communications skills should also be customized to specific audiences, such as executives, boards, internal auditors, sales and marketing professionals, and customers, among others. *But remember that all companies now have writing partners in large language models and GPTs, which should be leveraged.*

Verbal Communications Skills

The focus here is on experience making presentations that are easily understood and therefore actionable. *The key to verbal communications is also purposeful brevity*: is the team capable of such (verbal) communication? Verbal communications skills should also be customized to specific audiences, such as executives, boards, internal auditors, sales and marketing professionals and customers, among others.

Collaboration Skills

The focus here is on the ability to work productively with teams of all shapes and sizes. This ability requires experience and *soft* skills that integrate and optimize team contributions.

Persuasion and Negotiation Skills

The focus here is on the ability to persuade and negotiate in a zero-sum world. The most obvious capability is with internal constituencies regarding budgeting and external skills with investors. But the capability includes project prioritization and inter- and intra-group leadership, among anything that lives in a zero-sum world. No one can always win.

Presentation Skills

The focus here is on experience presenting to outside constituencies and stakeholders, especially vendors, external auditors, investors, customers and professional organizations. *Members of the team must be presentable to wide internal and external audiences.*

Drama Control

Drama is crippling to startups. Yet drama follows many start-ups because they're small, chaotic, unpredictable and vulnerable to product and market trends over which they have no control. Many startups are also comprised of younger professionals, which makes some teams more vulnerable to drama. More broadly, drama control defines a corporate culture that either becomes more-or-less dramatic. There must be some talent that manages the inevitable drama. But make damn sure you don't contribute to it.

Chaos Tolerance

Chaos is inevitable. The skillset necessary here is personality-based. Some of us can multitask but many of us cannot. Unpredictability is inevitable, but how you and your team deal with chaotic unpredictability is more important than many companies realize. The chaotic tolerance skill must be learned—because it's usually not innate. Said a little differently, don't panic when the wheels come off—because they will.

Regulatory Policy

You have to track the regulations that affect your startup—and there are lots of them. Some of the most important areas include privacy and surveillance, disinformation, compliance, fraud, cryptocurrency, antitrust, AI, and cybersecurity.

Regulatory policy is all around you. Some focus on the structure of the technology industry—like oligarchies—and some focus on specific issues—like privacy. Some policies focus on infrastructure—like Internet-for-All—and some on specific technologies—like AI. You should see policy as a threat *and* an opportunity. In fact, there are lots of start-up opportunities and constraints swirling around all of the regulatory areas. Track them; mine them.

Objectivity

This may be the toughest skill on the list to acquire and practice. Kool-Aid notwithstanding, many entrepreneurs believe anything and everything about themselves and their companies. They're biased in almost every way. Very few startups see themselves objectively, especially regarding their products and services or compared to their competitors. The ability to objectively assess products, services, technologies, teams, projects, competitors, investors, bankers, and lawyers is as valuable as any other skillset on the list. You will likely have to look outside for this skill, perhaps to members of your Board of Directors or your Advisory Board. If gaps exist—*and they always will*—you must act decisively to fill them.

Three Options: Repair, Rent, or Replace

The repair option is sometimes a good one: retrain and retool the willing keepers. Rethink how many full-time permanent professionals you really need: rent the others as "brawn" consultants, contractors, and long-term vendors. But always focus on the skills most important to your start-up mission.

CHAPTER 7

Building and Growing Startups

This chapter is about building and growing startups. There are a number of steps to growth, but only some of them are (somewhat) controllable: people, products and services, marketing and PR, sales, finances, structure, and happenstance, coincidence, opportunism, and luck. (You decide which are which.)

People

Well over a decade ago, I wrote a book called *IT's All About the People*. The book focused on the definitive role that humans play in the organization, management, and optimization of information technology in large enterprises. It was well received I think because of the subtitle: "*Technology Management That Overcomes Disaffected People, Stupid Processes and Deranged Corporate Cultures.*" Everyone is interested in *people*, everyone worries about people, and everyone depends upon people, especially entrepreneurs.

Growing a digital startup is also about people. Make sure that team members are suited to their roles. It's OK if some less emotionally stable ones code all day, but it's not OK if personality disorders infect your sales processes. Find talented people, remembering that there are a limited number of really good people, and an even smaller number of great ones.

Motivation is key: why are they on your team? Understand the motivation of all start-up team members—which better include a healthy dose of greed. Measure their performance, attitude, and collaborative quotients (CQs). ***Release human problem-makers at the*** *speed of light: they only get worse*. Prepare for the some of the *best* ones to abandon you for greener pastures.

As I reflect on the successful and unsuccessful teams I've seen over the years (including my own), it's clear the successful ones were comprised of complementary perspectives and capabilities. It's also clear that the unsuccessful ones were run by autocrats who believed until the end they knew best, and members of the team were just and only that—members of the team. Start-up teams are different from teams at companies like Cigna (or any large corporation). They must be staffed and managed differently, if *manage* is even the right word. *Partnership* is a better word. If *partners* fail to contribute—or are toxic—they should be removed as quickly as possible—because toxicity is contagious.

The question of start-up **culture** is as important as the skills and competencies of the people who comprise it. It's always important to understand the value proposition employees *believe* explains their employment. Why are they at your startup? Is it because they want autonomy? Is it because they want a fast career path? Is it just to make money? (It's likely all of these things, but mostly about money and the chance to get rich.) In my experience, start-up-ers like the casual—*and chaotic*—atmosphere, they like the opportunity to contribute directly to corporate outcomes, and they want to make some money as quickly as possible—*in reverse order*. The economy also has a lot to do with staffing startups. When times are tough, more talent is available to do *anything*, including working in startups. But these are not ideal start-up-ers. As soon as they can land a real job, they will leave. So build a list of people who like startups, who have worked at startups before, and who understand start-up cultures. Moving people from Cigna to start-up.com (a documentary about start-ups) is a horrible idea.

Another valuable insight refers to the *hero culture*, where individuals try to gather power and influence by flaunting their workaholism. This happens a lot because all startups live in interesting times when things change on an almost daily basis. Product, service, and market turmoil create fires that must be addressed quickly. A few leaders will rise to the occasion and put out the most dangerous fires. But firefighting is not a best practice; *heroism should not become status quo*.

Products and Services

Remember that whatever you're selling must be validated by market demand. Sure, there are companies that believe that you can offer products and services the market just doesn't understand it needs—yet. These companies tend to be well funded by true believers with time and money to burn. Chances are you're not one of those companies.

Your ongoing trends analyses will inform you about where the market is going and therefore where you need to be—except better, faster, and cheaper. Make sure you always watch the competition: only Apple could introduce a smart watch after smart watches were everywhere, though even Apple hasn't done so well with its late-to-market augmented reality headset, Vision Pro.

Learn to adapt: five-year product plans are ridiculous. Everything will change. Expect change; exploit change. Never design for longevity: you're just starting. How in the world can you develop a five-year plan? Instead, develop adaptation skills.

One of the earliest decisions you must make is about your ***product and service*** offerings. Are you selling a product, a service, or both? While you may believe this is a straightforward decision, I assure you it's not. How many times have you heard Kevin O'Leary on Shark Tank tell entrepreneurs they should not be selling a product or a service, but selling the IP or licensing the technology to others who might provide products or services based on the IP?

Many entrepreneurs begin with an idea—*a hypothesis*—about what the market needs and how they will satisfy the needs with just the right —differentiated—product or service. At ListenLogic, for example, we believed we should provide services to companies who wanted to track brand sentiment—expressed in social media—about their products and services. Companies wanted to know what their customers thought about their products and services, so they hired ListenLogic to listen to social media (and some other sources) on their behalf. Initially, this was a buy-versus-rent decision for our clients, as some clients debated the need for listening or hiring an outsider to listen on their behalf. Because listening was not that simple, the service we offered was attractive to clients. All good.

To deliver the service, we developed a methodology that was incarnated in a set of tools. Some of these tools were available off the shelf from other vendors, and some we customized. But as the methods and tools evolved, we found ourselves customizing more and more. Eventually, it appeared to make sense to develop our own proprietary social media listening platform. The idea was simple. We'd provide a service—social media analytics—and use our own software platform to deliver the service. We'd finance the development of the platform from revenue we generated from the service. We assumed the platform would give us competitive advantage, because some of our competitors had no proprietary tools at all, and if they did, we (of course) believed them to be inferior. So far, so good. But it was then decided to develop and sell a software platform as a software-as-a-service (SaaS) offering. The plan was to develop the platform with profits generated by ListenLogic and then go to market with a SaaS product that everyone could use to conduct social media listening and other applications.

Remember that selling consulting services is fundamentally different from selling software. While it may seem like a slight change, or even a good one, software development requires skills and competencies that consultants generally do not understand, let alone possess. This skills gap at ListenLogic required us to hire software engineers who were not co-located with the services team. In fact, the two teams were on opposite sides of the country, one outside of Philadelphia, Pennsylvania, and the other in San Jose, California. The east coast services team would develop requirements that the west coast team would implement with the east coast service team's money.

As time passed, the east coast services team—in order to respond quickly to client requests—began to look elsewhere for software solutions to their growing social media listening requirements. A not-so-little secret—confirmed by the president of ListenLogic at the time—was how infrequently the services team used the west coast platform to collect and analyze social media data. Instead, they used a variety of off-the-shelf tools to deliver services to their clients. This decoupled the east coast's requirements from the west coast's software development work—while the money still flowed west—something I failed to fully appreciate.

Over time, huge amounts of money from the services business was used to feed the growing appetite of the software team. The Board of Directors—of which I was a member at the time—grew increasingly concerned about all the money traveling west to build a software platform that the services team was not using to satisfy client requirements. Several board members expressed concern about all the siphoning which resulted in a huge, healthy board fight about the product-versus-service business model of the company. Some of the board members wanted to immediately stop funding the software platform and concentrate entirely on the services business, which was growing, though only slowly. Slow growth was attributed to lack of sales and marketing, which was the result of a lack of money (because money was sent west for software development!).

This was a strategic moment for the company—and one you should carefully analyze. Should ListenLogic be a product or service company? Or both? Should the team be consultants, software engineers, *or both?* The board fight was memorable (as many board fights can be) and resulted in board resignations and a reconstituted Board of Directors. But the outcome wasn't felt until ListenLogic and Akuda Labs became starved for cash.

The response was to ask the investors to write more checks. I was involved in that process and tried to raise additional funds for Listen-Logic and Akuda, but by this time, investors were hard to find. A few put in some additional money—including me—but many of the investors told me that they no longer believed the software investment made sense, so they refused to invest. Many of the investors also suffered from *investor fatigue* and told me that they did not believe in the company's two-directional strategy. This case is full of lessons.

Products or Services?

Which is right for your company?
While ListenLogic's margins were high, it was out of money. Neither business unit could make payroll. Bridge loans with generous terms

to make payroll were sought. What the dissenting board members predicted had come true.

I initially supported investments in the Akuda software platform development because I believed there was a longer-term opportunity in real-time unstructured data analytics and proprietary platforms to offer sophisticated analytics. But I withdrew my support and resigned from the board when I was unable to convince anyone that the Akuda platform ultimately had no future (based on assessments that were done by bankers, analysts at Accenture, and even a DARPA legend). I recommended that the software unit be shut down and ListenLogic be allowed to profitably grow with the services money it earned. I no longer believed the Akuda software development team could develop, deploy, and support a commercial software product in the highly competitive SaaS world—especially after the company's IB shared that he had called tons of companies about purchasing the initial software platform—and none of them was interested. At that point, I reasoned there was no future, and it was time to pull the plug on the software platform development project.

The (very well-documented) argument I made is important for all digital entrepreneurs to hear. I argued that no one at ListenLogic or Akuda had direct experience building and launching a commercial software product, that the world of software product management was a world basically unfamiliar to the east or west coast teams. I also argued that the competition was coming for us with deeper pockets and smarter engineers. While there were legitimate software rocket scientists on the west coast—who developed some interesting IP—none of them (based upon what I was told about the team) had ever taken a commercial software product to market. They had not created minimal viable products (MVPs) that successfully scaled. They were R&D people—par excellence—but not commercial software product developers. Nor did anyone in the company have experience selling software platforms or software services, or supporting commercial software products: no one had ever run a successful SaaS company. (Not to mention—again—that the market wasn't interested in what they were building.) But I was outvoted and off the board—which is precisely how these processes often work—and how they should work! Differences of opinion make the world go around. ***Outcomes decide which opinions are "right" or "wrong"—also as it should be.***

The investors threw their hands up in the air, consulted their attorneys, and ultimately just walked away after way too many email messages and late-night phone calls. It was a very sad ending to what was once a very exciting possibility. But these things happen—which is the point of discussing it here. Outcomes like what ListenLogic/Akuda experienced can be extremely instructive to entrepreneurs and investors.

Remember

- Bets are made all the time, but some bets are obviously better than others. Focus on what you know and do best. Resist the temptation to make wild bets. If you have a winning product or service business, conduct a ton of due diligence around switching from, or adding to, what's already working. Doubling-down is often the best strategy—until it's not. That's when pivoting makes sense. But make sure the pivot has been vetted as plan B—or C.

Implications?

- Make sure you understand the financial markets at the time of your launch. The markets will define your prospects for funding as your company grows, exit opportunities, and client abilities to buy your products and services. Once you have a bead on the market, adjust your strategy and tactics accordingly—but try to resist leaving the planet to do so.
- Make sure there's substance to your business model. Digital entrepreneurs should stay grounded, while opportunistic. (Yes, another conundrum.)
- The product/service challenge is a common one. It's also related to the oft-discussed *pivot*. Another conundrum? Sort of. Pivots

should be technology- and market-driven. ListenLogic and Akuda were competing with giants with deep pockets; the company was undersized and underfunded. The pivot to the development of a proprietary commercial software platform made some initial sense, but it became clear over time that the pivot was ill-advised, though by that time it was too late to raise more money to continue to test the hypothesis. While pivots are often necessary and sometimes even brilliant, they can also be dangerous, so pivot carefully.

The ListenLogic/Akuda case is not the only one that showcases the services versus products challenge. We looked at services at Coriell Life Sciences (briefly) to supplement the products we already offered. We looked at software products briefly at LiquidHub. I looked at products years ago at my company when we developed services around software requirements modeling. The idea was simple enough. We believed we could develop a *storyboard prototyping kit* that could be sold to software developers interested in modeling user requirements prior to software development. We developed a sample kit and discussed it with the Software Engineering Institute, software engineers, and our clients. No sale. It was considered overkill in the face of competing user requirements elicitation, modeling, and validation methods, tools, and techniques. So we killed the idea and continued to focus on services. In retrospect, I'm lucky the market was not encouraging, because I had no experience whatsoever developing "software kits."

LiquidHub, by the way, like all technology services companies, was always looking for new ways to define and deliver its professional services. I observed during a board meeting that the company was falling behind in its services offerings, or at least in the messaging around their offerings. As a traditional IT services company, LiquidHub found itself somewhat out of step with the market and their competitors who had already made the shift to all things digital. *The pivot was not from services-to-products but from services-to-additional-services.*

The lure of productization is often strong in services businesses because services are often enabled by methods, tools, and techniques. Why can't we, the reasoning goes, just turn the tools we already use into commercial products? The problem is—again—that the skills necessary to convert a set of methods, tools, and techniques into a commercial product are radically different from services skills. *Put another way, if your company is full of consultants, you cannot morph them into product developers.*

There's another step you should take to assess your products and services to determine if a product/service pivot makes sense. *You should continuously track your competitors' products and services* and how well—or poorly—those products and services are selling. If you're losing market share because your competition has a deeper products/services portfolio than you, you should look at their product/service mix and assess if their strategy might work for you—before the competition steals your too much of market share.

Finally, remember that *pivots from products-to-services are generally easier than pivots from services-to-products*. This is because product development is radically different from services, and expertise in product development is usually harder to find than services professionals. This is *not* to say that pivots-to-services are easy, but that services more naturally extend from products than the other way around. Product development also requires more money than service development with long product cycles that can change unpredictably. How many companies now offer AI, ML, and GenAI services that mysteriously just appeared as soon as market opportunities emerged? It's hard to offer a new commercial software product in ML or GenAI whenever you just feel like it, or when the Board of Directors tells you to look at productizing your services because someone at a cocktail party told them it makes sense.

Incubation and Acceleration

What about *incubation*?

Or *acceleration*?

Let's start with incubators, which support entrepreneurs at the earliest stages of their journey. Incubators provide (Cote, 2023):

- "Guidance on developing a product from your idea
- Help running experiments to prove product-market fit
- On-demand access to resources
- Legal consultation
- A workspace shared with other entrepreneurs
- Networking and mentorship opportunities
- Funding in return for a stake in your company (although many don't provide this)."

Accelerators, on the other hand, provide (Cote, 2023):

- "Funding in return for a stake in your company
- Immersive education on fundraising, product development, and growth marketing
- Access to an alumni network and investor connections
- Networking and bonding with your cohort
- Intensive mentorship from industry leaders."

Y Combinator is probably the most famous accelerator out there. But you have to apply, and like many of the VCs that moved downstream, accelerators are selective to improve their rates of success. If accepted, accelerators will often provide some cash and services for an equity stake in your company, which can range from 7 percent to 10 percent.

Can you just invent new products and services, like a new entrée on a menu? Unlikely. Nearly all the *accelerators* out there—with the possible exception of the picky Y Combinator—have low returns on their investments. There's research on the effectiveness of incubators (O'Brien, 2015; Fetsch, 2015). Fetsch analyzed the impact of incubators and found that *"incubated businesses do not outperform unincubated businesses ... overall, the difference in performance between incubated and unincubated businesses is 'marginal.'"* Other analyses report mixed outcomes (Gowder, 2023).

I'm not surprised by the findings. First, accelerators are selective. Not everyone gets support. If you look at the Y Combinator logos, for example, the business models of the companies they admitted to their program were already quasi-proven. It's like when colleges and universities tighten their admission standards to improve their rankings. You have to determine if you need help—which *can* be very useful—and if you will be accepted. You also have to think carefully about the equity you surrender.

I've seldom seen accelerators consistently churn out successful businesses, which is why I was always a little worried about Safeguard's incubator/accelerator, XL Vision. Over several years, Safeguard invested tens of millions of dollars in XL Vision. Based in Sabastian, Florida, at the time, XL Vision promised to develop new products and services. According to Safeguard's Annual Reports, over $60M was invested in XL Vision. When I arrived at Safeguard, I was introduced to XL Vision. By that time, Safeguard had already invested millions of dollars in the company. According to XL Vision's LinkedIn page, *"founded in 1993, this tech incubator created several startups, ChromaVision, Who?Vision, Integrated Visions, Presideo, and eMerge Interactive. XL Vision was acquired in 2001 by Venn-Works, Incorporated as XL Vision, LLC."*

Here's the XLT Vision business model as described in 2008 (XL Vision's model became XLT's business model after XL Vision was acquired and re-started as XLT TechGroup, Inc.)—Figure 7.1.

The always charismatic and brilliant CEO of XL Vision—John Scott —was interviewed in *Venture Catalyst: The Five Strategies For Explosive Corporate Growth* by Donald L. Laurie (2002). Here's what was said

XLT uses its own internally crated methodology, developed since 1993, which is based on a market-driven process, to create and develop new businesses from scratch. XLT does not commercialize IP or invest in other management teams. Exhibit 2 shows the five main steps of its process.

Exhibit 2: XLT Methodology Process

Step	Process	Reduces risk from
Discover	Identify large unmet market needs via corporate partners	Competition
Match	Source suitable technology solutions from technology partners	Technology development
Select	Select most promising combinations for company formation	Market adoption
Develop	Iteratively adapt combinations in the marketplace	Management
Scale	Scale new companies to commercially exploit the market need	Liquidity

Source: XL TechGroup Inc.

Figure 7.1 The XLT TechGroup methodology

about Safeguard's investment and the returns Safeguard received from its investments: *"after Safeguard Scientifics' initial investment of $8 million and a subsequent investment of $52 million to fund XL Vision, it earned a fortyfold return."*

Maybe it was there, but I couldn't find the forty-fold return in Safeguard's Annual Reports, but I did find: *"the methodology used at XL Vision by the XLT management team created over $1.1B in liquid assets for its principal shareholder Safeguard Scientifics from an investment of $157M, an annual IRR of 148 percent"* (Edison, 2008).

Lots of numbers: 40X? $8M? $52M? $2.4B? $157M? $1.1B? 148%?

It's hard to know what to know!

The incubator/accelerator concept is potentially powerful, but according to research is empirically weaker than perhaps many believe. That said, the concept still lives and in the hands of a few people can lead to success when lots of things are true—at the same time.

Takeaways?

- **Scheduled, programmed incubation or acceleration is a tough business despite how codified the incubation methodology might be**. Yet, the very idea of incubation and the appeal of prolific incubators is sometimes hard to resist, especially by investors looking for more action than their usual deal flow generates. But we know that the track record of incubation/acceleration is mixed (O'Brien, 2015; Fetsch, 2015; Gowder, 2023). So be careful not to be seduced by *incupreneurs*. Make sure the fit is right. Incubators and accelerators can be friendly, but they can also be expensive. As suggested, you should carefully decide if you want to team with incubators or accelerators. You have to determine if you really need help, if you will be accepted, and if the equity cost is worth it.
- Note, however, that there are different incubation/acceleration models out there. Y Combinator is somewhat different from

incubators/accelerators like XL Vision/XLT TechGroup (now Innventure), which attempts to commercialize from soup-to-nuts. Make sure you (as an entrepreneur or an investor) know who and what you're dealing with before you pull the trigger on any of the models.

- The XL Vision/XLT TechGroup methodology represents a different path to start-up success by essentially outsourcing innovation and commercialization to an organization that does it all. This methodology reduces the role of entrepreneurs as we're discussing them here, but can be a successful alternative accelerator.

My incubator/accelerator recommendation is to tread carefully. Much of what they provide—especially in the incubation phase—is what you should already be able to do. If you need help to just formulate ideas—the so-called ideation phase of innovation—there may be a larger problem with you start-up abilities. Accelerators, on the other hand, can provide capital and MVP/go-to-market support with an ecosystem you may not have. But they're expensive. So, pretend you're an investor in your own company: are accelerator investments and services worth the equity? Outsourcing innovation and execution to soup-to-nuts accelerators is expensive but can actually work with the right team. Deal terms here are complicated, so here too proceed with caution.

Marketing and PR

Form *and* content—and style *and* substance—are all necessary to announce your existence. ***Differentiation is now digital.*** The fastest, cheapest, and easiest way to reach customers is through the skilled use of digital platforms, digital content and digital transaction processing. It's important to use these platforms to employ a differentiate-among-many-strategy to pound the value proposition around your company's products and services. At a very basic level, you need to develop a core message. For example, are you a painkiller or a vitamin pill? Will you help your customers save money or make money—or both? Find the right style and substance, pound it, and then assess its effectiveness and adjust as necessary: marketing and PR are only as good as how well they're working.

First and foremost, clients and customers need to know you exist. Digital exposure is relatively easy and inexpensive. Derek Miller (2015) on entrepreneur.com offers *8 Digital-Marketing Tips for Bootstrapped Startups*:

1. "Be frequent and consistent
2. It's not about you, it's about your customer
3. Engage with your followers
4. Try small investments into the platforms
5. Critically think about your message
6. Find cheap and creative content
7. Optimize internal pages for conversions
8. Do outreach yourself"

Digital Advice

The key is the development of a **digital identity** that converts to revenue. Digital marketing and PR effectiveness will only improve over time (due to AI analytics), and their impact will crowd out other (traditional) marketing and PR campaigns. The world has changed. Demographics now predict success. But be careful about content creation. Not because it's not important or impactful, but because it can consume a ton of time and money. Blogs are addictive; copy is always late. Podcasts are better. In my experience, too many employees like to find a quiet place and post on the company's blog when they should be selling. So watch for content distractions or too many chefs in the logo, website, or blog kitchens. You also need to assess the value of speaking engagements, especially the ones across the country or on another continent. Make sure those speaking on behalf of the company are talented presenters. There's nothing worse than a mangled elegant message, so be brutal here. No one who finds direct eye contact uncomfortable should present to existing or prospective customers—or investors, for that matter. That said, a real or created speech can go viral for very little money.

GenAI can help you create marketing collateral with ease. *You must become facile with these tools—immediately* (McKinsey, 2023). Companies that master GenAI's contribution to marketing, PR, and all things buzz will win the optics war every time. There are countless tools that can help. How many of them do you know (Sell, 2024)?

Remember that marketing and PR are continuous core competencies. If your company's products, services, and brand are invisible or poorly communicated, you will fail. Like legal and accounting skills, you must become a master of at least the basics. Also remember to be flexible. When something works, do more of it, but when something fails, stop it ***immediately***. Find marketing and PR firms and independent consultants that will do the above for reasonable compensation. Avoid the large firms with lots of overhead that you pay for even if your projects are small. This may be one of the best times to find freelancers from Upwork, Guru, and 99designs, among other sites that link professionals with entrepreneurs (and other professionals). Finally, never forget how hard all this is. Marketing and PR are difficult and often unrewarding because their impact is hard to measure.

Most of the companies I've worked with failed to exploit the full range of available digital marketing and PR tools, and many of these companies were startups! While we can perhaps understand why old, large companies fail to package themselves as digital marketing mavens, how in the world could startups miss the opportunity to virtually display themselves? One reason is ignorance.

Another Is Fear

- Some entrepreneurs fear the process (and worry about the outcomes) because they've only experienced digital marketing as customers, not as creators. Their knowledge about the process, methods, and tools is shallow. If your knowledge about digital marketing and PR is limited, learn a lot and search for more. You cannot go slowly here, but at the same time, you don't need a full-time CMO either. The part-time help of an expert is what you need to launch. Are there differences of opinion here? Do many entrepreneurs want full-time CMOs? Some do, but there's a strong argument for *fractional* CMOs and other *fractional* professionals versus hiring full-time CMOs.[*]

- Most companies also change their message and their content way too frequently. Because the messaging and content creation tools make it easy to modify everything, many entrepreneurs cannot resist the temptation to make changes day after day. While change is good—I have consistently advised adaptation—not disruption—every few months.

- Startups need to go to market with a message that resonates with customers, and while that message should evolve over time, it's smarter to take a little more time to hone the message (and supporting content) than to release too early, only to have to quickly modify your identity shortly after you launch. Take the time to get the message as right as you can, recognizing that over time you will have to modify your market identity. You just don't want to make changes every month. Yes, another conundrum.

- *If there's any fear about GenAI's role here, seek immediate counseling. AI can do the easy **and** hard work—and do it all again in an afternoon.*

Sales

There's no more important start-up activity than sales: beg, borrow, steal, and buy as many customers as you can. Especially important are the initial lighthouse customers willing to testify to the power and greatness of your products and services. Buy as many lighthouses as you can find! Logo power is important to startups. Find as many recognizable (lighthouse and regular) customers you can find. *"We work for Amazon, Verizon and GM,"* is really good PR. (By the way, the more

---

[*]In fact, there are at least *12 reasons* why fractional professionals make the most sense for startups (Workfully, 2024).

well-known logos you land, the higher your valuation will be. Investors will pay for a chance to meet Jeff Bezos.)

Steps?

- Find salespersons with deep subject matter expertise. If you're selling analytics products or services, your salespersons should know a ton about analytics and the business domains to which they're selling.
- Performance matters more than words. Brutally track actual performance, not the elegance of promises or rigged benchmarking exercises.
- I'm a fan of giving away products and services to establish sales beach heads. While this is an expensive short-term strategy, it immediately gets your products and services into the marketplace. I gave away services early in my company's growth stage all the time. I also over-delivered—all the time—and made sure that my (paying) clients knew exactly what they were getting for free. We would routinely build storyboards of user requirements as loss-leaders to the kind of engagements we desperately wanted—and needed to survive.
- To make money, you must spend money. An old axiom, but a tough one for startups to practice. Products are easier to give away today, because they're generally hosted in the cloud where accounts can be set up for 30 days or so to allow prospective customers to play with what you've developed. If they like it, they will buy it; if they don't, they can help you understand why they didn't buy it. Value no matter what the outcome.
- If your products and services are content-related, it's especially easy to share them with prospective clients. If your products are complicated software platforms, for example, then the cost of sharing may be high, because you will have to train and support the trial if you want them to ultimately buy your product. All expensive, but all necessary.

- Start-up sales can be complicated. This is because your products and services will not be fully developed, and your go-to-market processes are anything but refined. No matter who you are, you will need help.

Overall Advice

- Selling as early as possible makes sense, though be careful not to oversell with an eager customer who wants your product or service tomorrow. Customer knowledge is always essential, but the best advice is to never pretend to be a large enterprise. The start-up–customer relationship is unique and should be managed accordingly. Expectations are appropriately different and can lead to long-term relationships—if you execute your first engagements well.
- Customer intimacy is much easier to achieve as a startup than as a large vendor selling just one more account. ***Sell intimately— while you're still small.***
- At the end of the day, sales processes should be formal, repeatable, and adaptive.
- Initially accept bad deals: you need to get on the map.
- ***Make absolutely certain that you know how to use GenAI tools to market your company. They will change the way you market and sell your products and services. You will pay dearly if you don't use these weapons.***

Develop sales process maps of your company (as well as the ones in which you plan to invest). Many companies want to digitally transform their business processes but have no idea where to start **because no one ever mapped the processes to be optimized!** Just as engineers require product maps, sales should command no less modeling respect.

- Remember that start-up selling is experimental. You won't know what works until it works. Test and measure different processes, scripts, and value propositions—and different salespersons.

- While you (as the CEO) may be wonderful (or not), you need to determine who on the team is also effective interacting with customers—and who's not. Can we be really honest here? Most people should not meet with customers. Find the ones with the right skills and competencies to develop relationships with paying customers. Be objective here.

- You should hire a fractional salesperson (or salespersons) with the right (subject matter) experience, the right touch, the right attitude, and the right motivation—that you have defined with just the right size stock grant (or no stock at all with performance grants). You should hire another fractional salesperson as soon as you get some sales traction. There's no better problem than keeping up with sales generated by more and more salespersons. ***Why fractional?*** Because you don't know how to sell your products or services until you start to sell your products and services. The learning curve will be steep and may or may not align with the talents of you salespersons or the capabilities of your products or services. In fact, it's unlikely they will unless there's an accidental match between your products, services and salespersons. ***Sales and marketing is a discovery process in the early days of your startup. Full-time commitments to CMOs and CFOs will likely require you to unravel relationships, compensation commitments and strategies and tactics you discover no longer work.***

Finances

I've talked about how to raise money. This is about managing the money you've raised. You need a go-to professional that your investors and customers will find credible. ***You*** also need ***daily*** eyes on the books. You especially need realistic worst-case revenue/expense projections (*best-case* projections are fantasies that panic-stricken entrepreneurs use to raise money from dumb Angels).

Allocation is another major issue entrepreneurs face:

- Startups should initially allocate most of their funds to product/service development and people. Once they launch, the ratio should balance to sales, marketing and delivery to lighthouse customers with long digital reaches—*even if that means that some product/service features go undeveloped.*

Let's agree again that startups don't need a full-time CFO: you need a fractional Certified Public Accountant (CPA) with a lot of start-up experience. But let's also agree that start-up financial management can be supported by an array of software tools that are inexpensive and scalable. But when all's said and done, you need to track several financial metrics that together comprise a financial management strategy.

Every investor and Board of Directors asks about cash flow. From every board seat I've occupied over the years, I've asked about cash flow and cash on hand—if the questions weren't preempted by the CEO's agenda (which they should have been). The key questions? *"What's the burn rate?" "How much runway do we have?"* Entrepreneurs must track burn and runway closely, and make sure the bills can be paid on time, especially payroll. Other questions board members will ask: *"What's the revenue, month over month?" "What about new business?" "When will we be profitable?" "When will we need more money?" "What logos did we land this quarter?" "Who are the competitors that scare you the most—and why?"* You must be able to answer these kinds of questions. Make sure you answer them quickly and honestly. *Never hide behind smoke and mirrors.* Trust is essential to your success. If your board and your investors don't trust you, or believe you're fast and loose with the truth, your tenure will be short.

The revenue question is the most challenging. *CEOs—including you—are usually delusional about revenue.* They hope against hope, believe in miracles, and always seem to believe they're going to find the white whale. I'm only exaggerating slightly. Just about every start-up CEO I've worked with over the years was delusional about revenue. Why do I say that? Because start-up CEOs only meet revenue targets about 10 percent of the time. It's always *"next quarter, revenue looks even better,"* as they summarize the chart that shows last quarter's revenue shortfall. ListenLogic, LiquidHub, Coriell Life Sciences, Safeguard, and just about everyone else all missed revenue targets (for one reason or another), and in every case, the CEOs were optimistic about the next quarter's revenue. *So remember when you're presenting to your board and investors that they really don't believe your revenue projections*, or at least they'll be substantially discounting your numbers. Board members will also calibrate you from the first meeting as a truth-teller or a sand-bagger. Be careful about what and how you communicate financial information. Directors know that revenue almost always flows slower than CEOs predict, that many customers are late payers, and multiple revenue streams are usually fantasies.

Revenue pipelines are also suspect. New business always takes longer than it takes, so the promising meeting you may have just had with a huge new customer may or may not ever amount to anything—and your board knows it. They assume your job is to present optimistic scenarios, but they're usually the realistic filters through which your numbers will be passed. Be careful here and watch your image, because you will be labeled as a *sandbagger, Don Quixote, the magician, the music man*, or much worse if you exaggerate all the time. There's a thin line between credibility and deception. ***Don't cross it.***

You will also be expected to have a revenue strategy. While revenue projections may be healthy, they may contract any number of diseases. So you will have to describe *Plan B* at every board meeting. *What-if* scenarios must be described in detail, and they must be assessed individually. The threat of external events is ever-present, and Boards of Directors will always worry about events that will impact the company. In those cases when board members are also investors, you can expect tough questions about revenue, profitability, and how you plan to respond to disasters, however unlikely you may believe they may be.

Repeat your standing offer to board members and investors at every board meeting to keep the company's books open for inspection. If you ever, ***ever*** refuse to open your books, you will immediately be accused of hiding information you don't want your board or your investors to see. At that moment, you will cross the red line between credibility and deception and forever change your relationship with key stakeholders and therefore the survival of your start-up.

As I've repeated over and over, entrepreneurs should open the books whenever any board member or investor asks. ***The obvious advice is across-the-board transparency.*** If you find yourself in arguments about what *transparency* means, or when it's *appropriate, necessary,* or *legally* required, you've completely missed the point. Transparency is not interpretable or nuanced around legal procedures and protections. You are either transparent or you're not.

Let's summarize

- Entrepreneurs must make sure that finances are well organized, well documented, and transparent with the help of part-time financial professionals with deep experience with startups. They should focus constantly on cash flow, burn rates, and runway. They should describe Plan B fundraising scenarios.
- Entrepreneurs should be transparent.
- Software tools can help with the organization and documentation of financial information.
- Personal character enables transparency.

Structure

Startups are presented in movies as open rooms filled with bright, quirky professionals happily working away all day and night on fun projects. When you watch these shows, it's hard to tell who's in charge. Reality is different. You need (loosely) defined roles with performance objectives and accountability. This does not mean that start-up organizational structures should be rigidly hierarchical. It does mean that *flat* still equals *accountable*. Perhaps more importantly, startups should manage to outcomes ***not*** processes: entrepreneurs should not care where or how team members achieve outcomes—so long as they're on time and excellent. Multitasking among small teams is an organizational strength: single-task specialists work at Walmart, Pfizer, Citibank, and Cigna.

There are some conundrums here. Startups are impetuous and agile. But they also need to run like businesses. Digital entrepreneurs must be of two minds. They must remain optimistic spokespersons and salespersons, and they must be professional managers. Sadly, in my experience, these two minds/bodies almost never exist in the same entrepreneur. So entrepreneurs—*you*—need help.

Entrepreneurs need a supporting cast of talented performers to get their companies off the ground. They need technologists, financial and legal professionals, sales and marketing professionals, and professionals capable of organizing and running a small organization. In larger companies, this would be the Chief Administrative Officer (CAO) or the Chief Operating Officer (COO). But you don't need a CAO or a COO. You need some structure and visible, empowered administrative roles filled by competent professionals.

What about reporting relationships? While start-up-ers need and want role flexibility, ***there must be an organizational structure***, even at the very beginning. This structure should recognize leadership and administrative roles, among other activities.

Let's look at some alternative structures (Wikipedia). Read about the structures and think about what your company does and how it should operate as a start-up.

Functional Structure

"One traditional way of organizing people is by function. Some common functions within an organization include production, marketing, human resources, and accounting. This organizing of specialization leads to operational efficiency where employees become specialists within their own realm of expertise. The most typical problem with a functional organizational structure is however that communication within the company can be rather rigid, making the organization slow and inflexible."

Divisional Structure

"The divisional structure or product structure consists of self-contained divisions. A division is a collection of functions which produce a product. It also utilizes a plan to compete and operate as a separate business or profit center. The advantage of divisional structure is that it uses delegated authority so the performance can be directly measured with each group."

Matrix Structure

"A matrix organization frequently uses teams of employees to accomplish work, in order to take advantage of the strengths, as well as make up for the weaknesses, of functional and decentralized forms. The matrix structure improves upon the 'silo' critique of functional management in that it diminishes the vertical structure of functional and creates a more horizontal structure which allows the spread of information across task boundaries to happen much quicker."

So how should you organize?

- Remember that you're small, so elaborate organizational structures make no sense. We can quickly dismiss functional and divisional structures.

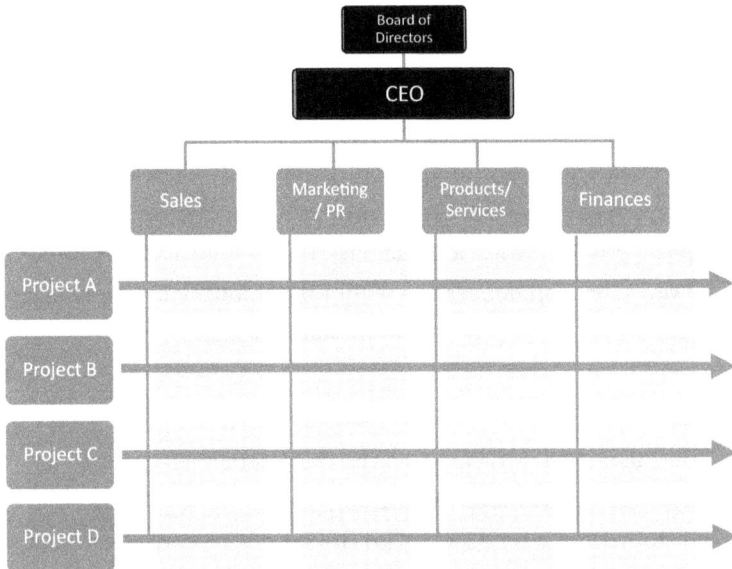

Figure 7.2 Project/function-driven organization

A matrix that describes a project/function-driven organizational structure.

- Startups can benefit from a matrix organization structure influenced by aspects of project/case/team/flat/virtual organizational structures.

When I think about start-up organizational structures, I think first about the must-have functions, like sales, marketing, finance, and product/service development, however fractional some of them might be. *I then think about the activities within these functions as projects.* I also think about shared responsibility across the functions and projects, though each function/project area has a leader, someone accountable for the projects that comprise the functions. Startups should structure themselves as project/function matrices, as suggested in Figure 7.2.

This structure assumes that partners will be working up, down, and across the organization. Because there are likely to be 10 or less people in the organization (with a few fractional professionals as well), double- and even triple-duty will be necessary. *But the main feature of the structure is that nothing occurs in a vacuum and projects drive progress.*

Some early projects would include product or service releases, branding, fundraising, sales presentations, marketing, and client management. All such projects should touch all the functional areas, which is what creates the necessary and appropriate start-up intimacy. Aspects of the structure can be virtual, and ideally, the culture of the organization is community-oriented. *In this structure, projects lead function.* In other words, professionals in the company have things to do—projects—and these projects define short-term corporate goals. Over time, as your company grows, you will need to adjust your organizational structure to accommodate the relocation of activity from projects to functions, where projects are subsumed within functional teams. *When* this change occurs depends upon each company. Note also that the role of the CEO changes over time. In a project-matrix structure, the CEO may well *own* specific projects or play the role of key team member of several projects.

When the company grows, the CEO will largely cease all this activity in favor or corporate-wide activities often defined as the major projects of each functional area, such as fundraising or major client/

customer management. The number of functions will also grow. Sales will separate from CRM and products/services will morph into R&D, innovation, IP management and other activities that keep the company's products and services *fresh* in the marketplace. You might even separate into separate business units (BUs) where each unit develops its own organizational structure. These changes are good because they assume revenue is growing.

The biggest mistake I've seen among the startups I've worked with and on whose boards I've served, is their failure to accept their start-up status. Too often they organize themselves as Fortune 500 companies with elaborate organizational structures and roles they actually attempted to fill. The assumption was they needed lots of different people performing lots of different roles (and collecting lots of different paychecks), and they would grow into the size they pretended they were. They sometimes—though not as often—made the opposite mistake: they failed to hire enough people to even keep the lights on.

Worse, many start-ups and early-stage companies I've seen change the organizational structures with late-night phone calls, when the CEO decides he (or she) no longer wants the sales team to report to the project leader and wants the sales team to report directly to the CEO. Or the CEO makes an arrangement with one of the professionals (like the fractional CFO) that constrains the behavior of that professional. For example, the CEO might order the CFO not to talk to investors or order the fractional general counsel to never answer any questions unless the CEO knows who asked the questions and why they asked them. This kind of behavior violates the project-matrix structure and the transparency principle in every way possible.

You should also listen to the team. There may be some good reasons why the structure you select is inadequate and even undermines progress. Keep the communication channels wide open and host (short) meetings once a week to discuss the strengths and weaknesses of your organizational structure and the processes it encourages. Some may be working fine, but some may be disastrous.

Here's some really good news:

- Just about everything you and your team do to run the business has been systematized in software. Digital marketing, CRM, financial reporting, expense reporting, email campaigning, project management, analytics, team communications, and training, among many other tasks, activities and functions are all available to digital entrepreneurs and their teams.

Lead generation, strategy, creative planning, data and analytics, customer support, distribution, automation and organization are cases in point, as Andrew Frawley (2022) explains so well in *StartupGRIND* and Tsosie, Rosenberg and Anthony (2023) provide lists of useful software tools.

The point?

- You can organize and manage yourself and your company with inexpensive business software. Many of these applications have become *standardized* not by some edict, but by adoption rates. For example, Dropbox is now a de facto storage standard simply because of the number of people who use the application every day.

Vendors you might examine include Zoho,[†] which offers a broad suite of applications for startups, early-stage companies, and small businesses. I have seen the suite in action in several startups. I have also looked at the suite's reviews—along with many of its competitors. You don't need expensive applications to run any aspect of your start-up.

Happenstance, Coincidence, Opportunism, and Luck

No one can predict anything, despite all the pundits, consultants, gurus, and (usually one-trick) successful entrepreneurs out there with home-made crystal balls. Things happen all the time that no one expects. Rather than stress over what might happen, learn to take blind shots

---

[†]I have no financial interest in Zoho or any of the companies mentioned here.

in stride. Entrepreneurs waste way too much time talking about what might happen—silly what-if analyses that defocus the team. If something's truly speculative, leave it alone. Learn how to quickly process new data, information, and knowledge, *not rumors, hearsay, or worse.* Better yet, learn how to exploit things that fall into your lap—and quickly manage unexpected (real) crises.

Incentives

There's one more issue you must address as a digital entrepreneur. It's a good one, by the way. Or at least it usually starts that way. You must decide how to incentivize and hopefully reward your founding team with shares in your company. There are at least two ways to do this. The first way is to award preferred shares to key members of the team. The second is to grant common shares or options to purchase common shares. Preferred share grants are the best gift you can give employees. Common shares are OK, but not nearly as good as preferred shares. Options are the least generous because they vest over time. There are also restricted stock units (RSUs), restricted stock awards, and even stock appreciation rights, which may be vested or unvested.

We discussed this in the context of investor term sheets. Just as investors want preferred shares, so do employees. Preferred shareholders get their money first whenever there's a distribution (or, hopefully not, a liquidation) of funds. Common shareholders wait in line.

But how much should you give to incentivize the team? How many preferred shares, common shares, or options should you grant? What classes of stock should be granted? One formula for start-up equity-sharing is preferred stock for founders and investors and common stock and stock options for employees. But there are no hard-and-fast rules around the practice. Because preferred stock is the most valuable stock, why not share some of it with key employees? Same for founders: why should they just get common shares? The potentially least valuable shares are stock options, because those who hold options must sell their shares back to the company to make money, and the only time that makes the option holder money is when the value of the stock rises considerably—

or when the company is sold and the options vest automatically (if that's the deal).

The argument for the traditional formula is based upon the assumption that all stock classes will be in the money because the company will succeed. But remember that 90 percent of startups fail. The only shareholders that make money (or usually only get their money back if the company dies) are the preferred shareholders. Preferred shareholders of course argue that they're the ones who founded the company or wrote the checks to launch and support the company, so they should get whatever's left if the company fails. The founding employees argue that it's unfair for them to work 80 hours a week for a few years and receive nothing for years of their professional lives.

There are some more or less standard allocation models. Here's one that's pretty typical organized around the different categories of stock (Stripe, 2023):

- **"Common** … (for) founders and employees … (with) … dividends or proceeds from a sale of the company.
- **Preferred** … (for) investors … (with) … first entitlements on dividends and assets if the company is liquidated.
- **Options** … employees (get) the opportunity to buy shares at a set price within a designated period.
- **Restricted stock units** … a promise to award a … shares … dependent on meeting specific conditions such as staying with the company for a set time or hitting performance targets.
- **Warrants** … typically given to investors, allowing them to purchase shares at a specific price."

The philosophy I'm advocating is a generous one. Given the risks around start-up survival, founding employees should be treated as close to investors and founders as possible. There are tax-advantaged ways to treat partners like investors. But so-called RSUs keep investors and partners at opposite ends of the generosity scale. "Incentive stock options" (ISOs) are better but still not overly generous, at least not in my view. Also good are (immediately exercised) nonqualified stock options. Both forms of equity are not taxed as ordinary income, should a gain occur.

So:

- There are multiple classes of stock in a company. You need a philosophy and an attorney to map the strengths and weaknesses of each class. My philosophy is clearly on the generous side—for some. You can decide for yourself, but if you want to motivate your team, give them a meaningful piece of the company. Remember: follow the money. Because everyone does.

CHAPTER 8

Exiting Startups

Remember that no one wants to buy startups unless the company has killer IP or lists of recurring customers. Profitable recurring revenue is nirvana. Exits occur when a startup becomes empirically successful.

Good exit zones assume success. Bad ones assume failure. Three of the seven exit outcomes are horrible or just OK; four are solid or amazing. There are variations of all seven exit scenarios. But by and large, if you profitably grow, someone will be interested in helping you grow to the next level, and if you continue to profitably grow, someone will want to own you.

It's also important to think about the kind of exit that would excite you the most. Some entrepreneurs are sprinters, while others are long-distance runners. Sprinters are less interested in lifestyle outcomes than they are in outright acquisitions. Some entrepreneurs want nothing to do with running a public company or even serving in one. Exits should be assessed at the beginning. Dreaming drives motivation.

Exit Zones

Exit strategies are driven 100 percent by where you find yourself after you've tested the market and after the market has spoken to you about (1) your products and services and (2) about the trends and trajectories in which you're participating. You also need to speak directly to yourself about your ability to execute and participate in your targeted markets. You need to ask the man or woman in the mirror about short-term versus longer-term execution. Can you scale?

Exit outcomes can take several forms depending on where your company is along the start-up timeline. If execution has been weak, then your exit outcome will be modest—if there's an exit at all. If, on the other hand, you've got hockey stick growth—and you are strategically aligned with your market—your exit can be generous.

Outcomes are directly tied to performance. If you go bankrupt or your team is acqui-hired, you have failed, and you will likely have some explaining to do to your team and especially your investors (should you choose to speak with them). IP exits *can* be fine if the strategic valuation is high; much better if your patents are granted versus pending. Remember that the value of IP is industry-dependent where some industries, like biotech, will often pay more for strategic IP than some other industries.

Recapitalizations define relief for entrepreneurs and their founding investors. They represent a way to take money off the table at an acceptable valuation. Some companies gather more steam than even entrepreneurs expect. They generate real profit! Sometimes these companies are at their best when they just generate cash-for-the-taking. But selling your company to the highest bidder at the highest strategic valuation possible generally produces significant wealth for everyone involved. Only an IPO can generate more long-term returns to the founders and initial investors, though that's not always the case either: IPOs can fail.

Entrepreneurs must make sure their team and investors are managed and informed throughout the start-up process. That's easy when the returns on investments are healthy but daunting if you've failed to at least return original investments to your investors. That's because at the end of the day, entrepreneurs are responsible and accountable to the investors who wrote checks as acts of faith and trust in what they were sold as the next great thing. When the wheels come off, there's a ton of explaining to do, and even more reputations to repair. So entrepreneurs need to be extremely careful and diligent about the building process. If they fail to build, they will fail to return any money to their investors, and if they fail to return any money to their investors, they're unlikely to persuade those investors to dine with them again, no matter how tasty the digital treats might be.

The old saying—*"hope for the best, but plan for the worst"*—applies here. Entrepreneurs should work toward—and away from—"zones," as described below.

The Dead Zone

- Worst exit: bankruptcy. Remember that it's more likely you will lose everything than become rich, so when that day arrives, accept it professionally and ethically if you can (and not all entrepreneurs can). Remember your reputation and legacy are at stake. If you end your entrepreneurial journey badly, no one will ever forget, and while you may rise from the dead with a little help from your friends, you will forever display the bankruptcy tattoo. So if bankruptcy happens, manage it carefully. Most importantly, take responsibility for your actions: no one likes a sore loser or someone who always looks for someone else to blame for his or her failures.
- Horrible exit: acqui-hire, where your team is sold to the highest bidder for pennies on the dollar. Sometimes this is the best you can do. Your products and services may have failed, but your team is solid—and therefore desirable, especially if their skills are in white-hot technology areas. Acquirers will offer you money and stock for these people, but everyone will have to create some attractive stay packages, which usually consist of bonuses paid to key people to retain their services for some fixed period of time.

The Near-Dead Zone

- Weak exit: an IP-only sale, where your pending IP is sold to the highest bidder for a negotiated (OK) operational or (better) strategic value. This is also a less than ideal outcome for you and your investors, but at least there's something for everyone to sell. IP valuation is extremely subjective and volatile: what an acquirer might find valuable today, they might deem worthless tomorrow. The challenge is timing. Given the pace of technology change, by the time a patent may be granted, it's likely that someone else has already developed something better/faster/ cheaper. On the other hand, if you're selling a company with products in the marketplace based on a unique, patented technology, there may be some value. Try to be objective and seek continuous advice about the current and future value of your IP.

The Comfort Zone

- Solid exit: recapitalization, where your company is purchased by outside investors at a negotiated value that results in a buyout for the founders and Angel investors at some multiple of the initial valuation of the company. This is a good outcome for some founders and investors, especially if a lot of time has passed between the founding of the company and the recap offer. Partial or full liquidation opportunities also help quell investor unrest, which always grows as time passes: the longer it takes for investors to monetize their investments, the angrier they become, especially if there's been relatively little communication with investors after they've written their checks.
- Good exit: lifestyle-cash-extraction, where management and investors suck as much cash as they can—for as long as they can—from a successful ongoing business. This good exit is not a real exit but the realization that the business may be a cash cow capable of yielding milk every quarter. If you want to see this in real time, go to the Web and track insider transactions. Find the stocks that have traded in narrow ranges for years and how much money investors and management are taking off the table on monthly or quarterly bases. What's going on? They're extracting cash from the company on a scheduled basis. After they've taken as much money they want or need off the table, they may pivot to a sale. If you're lucky enough to have this problem—scheduled cash extractions versus selling the company —you're in a good place.

The End Zone

- (Excellent exit): strategic acquisition by a company that believes your business (revenue and customers) adds financial and (ideally) strategic value to their existing portfolio of products and services. This is your goal, especially if the valuation is strategic. Some companies and technologies are acquired for incredible valuations, like the $2B Facebook paid for Oculus Rift. More typically, companies are acquired because there's both operational and strategic value.

- (Best exit): an Initial Public Offering (IPO), where shares of your company are sold to institutions and the public. While this exit is a dream for many entrepreneurs, it essentially represents the sale of your company to strangers willing be bet on your future. If you're lucky enough to take a company public, sell enough stock to offset all the work you did to make the company desirable – and then some. You don't need to tell your investors to sell: they will unload as much of their stock as soon as they can, at least that's what the data tells us.

What do you think? Is comfort enough?

Or will you only be happy if you score?

CHAPTER 9

Conclusions

A book like this should draw some useful conclusions and offer some good advice. The best way to do this is to list the *takeaways*—the essential messages about the start-up process.

First, ask yourself if you really want to launch a startup and if you have the right stuff to endure the slings and arrows from the people and the process. If you do, there are some things you should do to launch and, against the odds, succeed. Remember the process is exhilarating, terrifying, expensive, and abusive. It can also make your very rich. Or very poor. It can make you some new friends. It can lose you some old ones. So before you begin, take a good, hard look in the mirror. If you nod, you're there. If you grimace, maybe not.

So here they are. Some lessons and advice from the trenches. My trenches, for sure, but others as well. Read them and weep, smile, laugh, or just nod.

Takeaways

People Takeaways

- Measure the subject matter distance across entrepreneurial experiences. If serial entrepreneurs move from dentistry to digital to dermatology, they're not serial entrepreneurs—they're *wannapreneurs* or *opportuneurs*, trends chasers looking to cash in on what someone said at a wine-tasting party was an opportunity to make some quick money.
- On the other hand, if they have a portfolio of similar successful and unsuccessful entrepreneurial experiences, they are SMEs who should be taken more seriously.
- Hopefully, you're an SME and not an opportuneur.

- Be very wary of overly glib entrepreneurs who believe they can sell anything. Or build anything. Or manage anything. No one does everything well.
- Facts often don't matter. Accept it. It's all about power and control, so make sure you acquire more than enough power and control to nurture and protect your baby—regardless if you're an entrepreneur or an investor.
- Successful means profits, IP, acquisitions, mergers, and IPOs. Anything and everything else is spin—no matter how many great stories they tell—or people they blame for their misfortunes.
- Also, beware of resumes with lots of one year gigs and lots of board seats that stay warm for only a year or two. This kind of mobility is a red flag: if an entrepreneur is so smart, why is he or she moving around all the time?
- Not all entrepreneurs are creative. Many do not have even the most basic or obvious skills and competencies to be credible, but some of them bring other things to the table, like personal connections, name recognition, and, therefore, the ability to connect people with money (with firm handshakes and great smiles).
- Don't become frustrated. There are many characters in this movie playing different roles. Some are interesting, and some are instantly forgotten. But in a well-developed script, all can be exploited. As you develop your entrepreneurial instincts, make sure you learn how to categorize the players. Also learn to suffer fools well—and quickly. This skill is necessary in a world with way too many fools and frauds. You know what I mean. No, you must acknowledge that there's nothing you can do about fools and frauds—except exploit, marginalize, or avoid them.
- There's not much to be gained from complaining endlessly about how ridiculous the questions at a pitch meeting are, how clueless the people in charge are, or how they ascended to positions of power and influence. Entrepreneurs need money, teams, and partners. They seldom find all three in a single package.

- Self-awareness is one of the most important personality traits an entrepreneur can have. If an entrepreneur has no idea what people think about his or her abilities or performance, then the entrepreneur—perhaps you—will fail.
- If someone performance benchmarked you, what would they discover? Do you know what you do well and poorly? You also need to know who you really are and how you're perceived: are you really an entrepreneur or do you just play one on TV?
- The passion that many investors insist upon is easily faked: passion—whatever that even means—is way, way overrated, especially if it's compared to plans developed by experienced, successful, flexible entrepreneurs. I'll take the experienced, successful entrepreneur every time over the brand new, "passionate" one.
- The display of passion is, however, necessary because investors have passion on their due diligence checklist, not because it predicts to success, but because they need to tell everyone at the Monday morning investment committee meeting that the entrepreneur is passionate. So you have no choice but to display it, even if you're not all that passionate. (Remember that passion is not a substitute for intelligence or knowledge.)

Investor Takeaways

- The goal of seed financing is survival. If you survive for six months, you may live to explore the possibility of longer-term success. But note that success is predicated upon revenue growth: if growth sputters, you will fail—even if you're able to convince investors to keep writing checks. The financing cycle overweighs the importance of revenue growth—so pursue revenue relentlessly.
- Do not take any money from friends—ever—unless you're prepared for the friendships to die-over-money, which many Angel friendships do.

- Do not offer entrepreneurial friends money—ever—unless you're prepared for the friendship to die-over-money, which many Angel friendships do.
- Do not take money from members of your family. There's very little difference between friends-and-money and family-and-money. Both relationships are likely to end badly.
- Do not take money from friends of friends or extended family members you only see at weddings and funerals.
- Never, ever take money from people who cannot afford to lose all or most of the money (even if they're so-called accredited investors). Do not take money because someone loves you or might feel guilty if they refused to fund your new idea.

Angel Takeaways

- If you cannot self-fund, turn to professional (not dumb) Angels and expect to sell a meaningful part of your company to your seed investors. You can also turn to debt and your co-founders for funding. Even your founding Board of Directors can be targeted for seed funding.
- While stupidity can be appealing, eventually you will pay the price. So avoid dumb Angels as consistently and steadfastly as you avoid taking money from friends and family.
- The ideal Angel is disciplined and experienced, especially in your business domain.
- It's important for entrepreneurs to respect their investors and speak with them often and make certain that these communications are open and consistent. Beware of entrepreneurs who avoid frequent group communications. Some entrepreneurs—I hope not you—prefer a *divide-and-conquer* approach to investor communications. This approach allows entrepreneurs to describe different realities to different investors at different times. But it's only a matter of time until the realities collide.
- If you're the entrepreneur, please keep communications open, consistent, specific, frequent, and scheduled. Don't cause worlds

to collide. Remember that your Angel investors comprise the bank, and it's not good business to anger the bank—especially because you may well need additional money from the same investors.

- One way to avoid *investor fatigue* is to keep your Angels happy, and the best way to do that is to keep them informed. You must also assume that your Angel investors will communicate among themselves. So communicate openly with all of them consistently. The last thing you want is Angel distrust or the discovery that Angels are receiving different messages from you or your team. There is no faster path toward Angel investor activism (and lawsuits) than investor isolation or confusion.

- Angels fly around at various locations. You can find them on AngelList, the Keiretsu Forum, Gust, the US Angel Investment Network and the Angel Capital Association. They're everywhere.

VC Takeaways

- VCs know what they know and not much else. Many VCs are self-assured because they have money to invest, because they're rich, and because entrepreneurs are always asking them for money. They're not self-assured because of their innate intelligence or their technology domain expertise. They are bankers in every sense of the colloquial use of the term.

- Most of the success that VCs enjoy is due to their relationships and what many of them describe as their instincts. Most of their success therefore is the result of who they know, not what they know or what they do. It's amazing how much VCs rely on the judgments and work of others to do their jobs. Without their networks, associates, consultants, and relationships, many of them would be incredibly ineffective. Entrepreneurs need to understand all this before engaging VCs to conduct due diligence on their company's technology or digital business model for potential investment purposes.

- One of the requirements of this knowledge gap is that you must speak two languages—venture-speak and tech-speak. Do not get into the technology weeds with Managing Directors or Partners of the VC funds from which you might want funding. (Get into the weeds with Associates and Interns if they're leading due diligence efforts.) Talk venture-speak with Managing Directors and Partners, before or after you talk tech-speak with the due diligence people. Then, well, you get the idea.

- Your VC due diligence should focus first on who the VC knows, and with whom they invest, work, travel, and win. Look for relationship pedigrees that include major law firms, successful entrepreneurial testimonials, and happy institutional investors.

- Interview entrepreneurs who have worked with VCs in the past. Determine their value as partners. Play golf, chess, or poker with VCs and everyone you can find in their personal and professional orbits. Let them win.

- Interview entrepreneurs who have worked with the VCs you are considering (just as they will interview witnesses to your track record).

- While VCs win whether they succeed or fail, you need to know what the empirical record shows, not lore or hearsay, but actual results, like the IRR of every fund they've raised. Take no prisoners here: this is the most important VC due diligence you will ever do. Find out a lot about them on PitchBook and learn your way around VentureBeat, CBInsights, and the National Venture Capital Association, among other databases, that report and comment on the entrepreneurial money-lending business.

- Inspect VC performance across the sectors where they place their bets. Some firms are much better at biotech than IT services. Where is your company? Match the VC firm's best performance sector with your company's sector.

- Assess the firm's orientation—is it an entrepreneur-friendly firm or a firm that focuses primarily on its Managing Partners and investors? There are strengths and weaknesses with each bias, but remember that entrepreneur-friendly firms have better deal flow than firms that have firm biases, and you'll have more flexibility with entrepreneur-friendly firms.

- There is no more deadly combination than arrogance and stupidity. If you see this combination, run. You do not want their money even if it's cheap. They will be impossible partners.
- It's important to calibrate the integrity and ethics of VC firms.
- Are VCs a last resort? The only time you should seek VC funding is from a position of strength—when the VCs want you—not the other way around!
- If you chase VCs for money, they will give you as little as they can for as much of your company as they can own. If you're financially weak, they will crush the valuation of your company. Why? Because they can—and because weakness is red meat to VCs. Always remember why VCs exist—and it's not to make you happy, create jobs, or contribute to the community. No matter how many charity balls they attend, how friendly they are, or how many political candidates they back, they are one-celled organisms in constant search of more, and more (and more) money for themselves and their investors—in that order.
- Know your investors and understand their tolerance for risk long before you speak with them. Make sure you match your performance with their investment criteria, and make sure you're aligned with their exit expectations. If not, then you might end up in a fight with your principal investor about when and how to sell your company, or when to raise more money. This is a fight you want to avoid.
- The lower the risk tolerance, the higher the valuation the investor should pay. This is simply because investors must pay for lower risk—which professional investors (and seasoned entrepreneurs) understand all too well. If your company is downstream and revenue/profit positive, you're expensive.
- Where are you, where is your company, and what are your VC options and targets? What kind of market are you in? Do you know? Make sure there's a match.
- Listen to economic recession forecasters because the value of your company will rise and fall with the state of national and global economies. Are you an *A* entrepreneur or a *B* or *C* player?

Be honest with yourself, your team, and your investors—and
seek players at the same level.

- Warm introductions are always better then cold calls. Cold ones
—like crowdfunding, other forms of online financing and cold
calls—seldom, if ever, generate meaningful funding, and even if
it does, it will take forever.

- *A* player money is more expensive than *B* or *C* player money.
They will take more equity simply because A players can take
more equity; B and C players will accept less equity for the same
amount of money because they have more limited deal flow—
but A players have the best relationships. You get what you pay
for.

- Remember that venture capital investments are gambles against
the house. While this is not your concern as an entrepreneur
it's important to understand the motivations of your venture
partners and even their investors. VCs invest in many companies
hoping one of them will be the unicorn (or something approach-
ing unicorn status) that makes their fund. You must track your
position in a fund that invests in your company. If you're in
the *maybe-a-unicorn* category, you're OK. But if you fall into
the *probably-a-loser* category, you need to prepare for some time
in the desert. Remember also that venture funds have a 10-year
life span, with the possibility of a two-year extension. Knowing
where your investment falls along that timeline is important. It's
better to be at the beginning of a fund's lifespan than at the end.

- At the end of the day, it's important for entrepreneurs to fully
understand the venture capital business because it's not what it
seems—or what VCs want their investors or entrepreneurs to
believe.

Legal Takeaways

- Managing legal counsel is a survival skill. But you may have
had only limited exposure to law firms and venture attorneys—
which makes you vulnerable to their tricks. One approach is to

seek second opinions on all things legal. The opinions should involve fees, time, and prioritization as well as alternative legal strategies. Free advice from your divorce attorney's brother-in-law is dangerous.

- Negotiate alternative fee structures beyond hourly fees.
- You should develop metrics for legal performance. How long, and for how much money, does it take your lawyers to get things done? Who are the most efficient lawyers—and which ones are terrible? Which demeanor is most compatible with your team and your style, and which ones do you never want to meet again? Timeliness is a critical metric. If your attorneys are unresponsive when you need them the most, replace them.
- Because the legal world is so tangled, make sure your lawyers are not directly or indirectly conflicted. If they are, fire them.
- Finally, startups should never pay retainers. They should pay by the drink.

Investment Banker Takeaways

- Lawyers and IBs—like D&O insurance and lawyers—are necessary evils. They have nothing to do with your technology offerings or your team's ability to develop a CustomGPT. But they require as much attention as your technical team and the products and services you're developing.
- Do not completely abdicate the management of the legal/banking team to your part-time CFO or your part-time in-house general counsel. You must educate yourself. I realize this sounds onerous—and it is. But the alternative is to remain ignorant about issues that if mishandled can cost you money, time, and market competitiveness. For example, what if your IP attorney is slow and incompetent?
- Finally, beware of *good guy* references. I cannot tell you how many times I've worked with professionals who were described as *good guys* who turned out to be incompetent, unresponsive, rude

and worse. By all means, accept *good guy* suggestions, but before hiring *good guys*, be sure they're *professional*.

- All of that said, if you must beg an IB to work with you—unless you are fire-selling your company—you're probably misaligned with the outcome you want: you want to optimize a situation and they want to kill-and-eat as quickly as possible. Bankers want to make money and publicize their *wins*, so if you cannot make them rich and famous, they will avoid you—unless they are bad IBs. So be careful here. Like with VCs, the best time to contact IBs is from a position of strength, never weakness. If you're weak and you want out, then hire an IB to dump your company—and just look away. They might succeed and get you a little money. Or they might fail. But lower your expectations about transparency and the purity of the process.

Boards of Directors Takeaways

- CEOs and lead Angel or institutional investors often don't want objective advice, *especially if the advice suggests that major changes should be made to the company's strategy and tactics.* While we could debate the merits of stubbornness, many *founders and their founding investors are often way too sure of their strategies and therefore unwilling to listen to contrarians.*

- CEOs are *often blind to real competition and market trajectories.* The conviction and passion that enabled them to start the company also often prevent them from pivoting. Directors—especially *independent* Directors—can help a lot: find them.

- Board *politics can be brutal,* especially when board members have personal relationships with management and—worse—investors. Many board members are drive-by Directors, who read company quarterly reports on the way to the board meeting, if they read them at all. You can easily spot the ones who prepare and those who don't: remember the advice about suffering fools well?

- Make sure your company's OA speaks directly and purposely to board responsibilities, board election processes, and board composition. This is standard fare in OAs, but read it carefully. As the founder-entrepreneur, you want some flexibility, but your investors will want protection from worst board practices. Your auto-default should be investor-friendly language and guidelines.

- Do a requirements analysis: what board skills and competencies do you need? Recruit and staff accordingly—even within investor constraints (which will be formidable). Use the skills and competencies argument to assuage investor pressure about who should sit on your board.

- Keep the number of board members initially to three; expand as necessary and required (when you receive institutional and corporate money). Five is obviously more manageable than seven: the larger the board, the more intra-board problems. That said, investors are routinely granted board seats in exchange for investments, but pay special attention to the tiebreaker, the fifth, seventh, or ninth seat, which should be a true *independent* director. You should not cede control of the tie-breaking board seat to the investors. If you do, you may lose control of your company.

- Boards are inherently political: plan for it—but don't fuel it. Humans cannot avoid tension and conflict, especially when vested financial interests clash, like when the founding Directors clash with the new Series A Directors. Personalities are extremely important to board management (and politics). While many of us resist *EQ*-based performance calculi, personalities that blend are far better than those that clash. Interview proposed investor Directors. If you find obvious problems, address them immediately.

- Communicate openly, consistently, simultaneously, and frequently with your Directors. Do not divide and conquer. It will backfire. Provide whatever materials board members request —including, obviously, financial records. A best practice—if you're large enough—is to have your CFO report to the board every quarter on the financial status of the company.

- Task your Directors. Ask them to sit on various committees (again, assuming you're large enough) and ask committee chairpersons to help with specific projects, even if the *projects* only consist of making phone calls, sending emails, or texting. Directors can be a great source of talent as well, which you will need as your company grows.
- Be organized: schedule board meetings way in advance; call, as required, impromptu board meetings. Agendas (and all supporting materials) should be shared at least a week in advance of board meetings. Open data rooms for Directors to browse board meeting materials, company documents, and financial statements. Keep the rooms open.
- Listen to your board: Directors are there to watch and help. Ask them to check your thinking, your organizational structure, your go-to-market strategy, your competitive intelligence, and your team—among other operational and strategic initiatives about which you need objective eyes. Pitch them; practice with them. Many Directors have sat in your seat and therefore have a good understanding of your role, challenges, and opportunities.
- Pay close attention to your timeline. Startups need different skills and levels of engagement than early- or later-stage companies. Watch your company. When you transition from one status to another, rethink your board requirements. An infusion of cash will always require you to rethink your board, but you should proactively anticipate board reaction to market shifts, competitor pivots, cash burn, and staff challenges which will occur on a regular basis.
- Remember your board has a fiduciary responsibility to the shareholders—not you, except in your role as a shareholder.

Advisory Board Takeaways

- Advisory Boards can be pro forma or specifically tasked with projects. They tend to be PR vehicles intended to raise a company's profile through a network of professionals that might help the company with warm introductions and informal advice.

- Leverage Advisory Boards by filling them with big brands, celebrities (if possible), pundits, financiers, prominent attorneys and even an academic or two—all for the purpose of raising the profile of the company.
- You might even recruit an Advisory Board member or two onto the Board of Directors as your corporate status changes.

Whole Team Takeaways

- You need to understand all the players before you invest your life savings and total psyche into your great idea.
- You need to understand the real start-up process and the players that can help you, the players that will hurt you, and the players you may never even see. It's up to you to come to this game prepared.
- Even if you're never asked, make sure your investors see everything, warts, and all, and don't just show them where the landmines are. Remove them, and then present them to your investors regardless of their size and potential lethality. This is consistent with the transparency best practice. If you find yourself happy about the questions the due diligence team didn't ask, you've violated the transparency best practice.

Technology Trends Takeaways

- Do you (and your investors) understand macro versus enabling technology trends?
- Is everyone tracking M&A activity as insight into technology trends?
- Entrepreneurs should understand the domains in which they work.
- Investors should also have at least a basic understanding of the technologies in which they invest, though as noted, they often don't.

- If you detect ignorance, prepare to lecture—but not too condescendingly lest you offend a rich, insecure investor.
- Everyone in your entrepreneurial orbit should appreciate macro technology trends.
- Technology entrepreneurs—you—must understand macro and enabling technology trends as well as the M&A activity that accelerates and validates the trends. You need to locate your innovative technology with specific reference to competing technologies.
- Do not expect investors, bankers, or lawyers to understand much of anything about macro or enabling technology trends. They will, however, know something about M&A transactions, because their teams track technology transactions that affect their ability to exit their investments. It is one of their key valuation metrics.
- If you're an entrepreneur incapable of understanding macro and enabling technology trends, you're not an authentic technology entrepreneur. You need to surround yourself with technologists, though you will never be able to validate their insights.
- ***The most important trend you should track is GenAI.***

Pitch Takeaways

- Prepare *the pitch*: understand the form and content that investors expect. Ask those who have presented to your investors to solicit their ideas about what works and what doesn't. Ask the investors (prior to the pitch) directly what they want to hear and how they'd like to hear it. Ask how much time you have. Ask about the *must knows*, and always ask about what infuriates them most about entrepreneur pitches.
- *Prepare for the unexpected and be flexible.* Make sure that whoever is making the pitch is smart, articulate, and confident—but never arrogant. Do the drill: pick one or two slides that say it all.
- The pitch itself must be *active*. It cannot consist of 25 dead PowerPoint slides with tons of text and graphics on every slide.

By this time, everyone expects pitches to be brief and to the point aligned ideally to the audience's catechism. It should have links to graphics and videos with an embedded use case-based demonstration. A prospective client's testimonial is effective and usually obligatory. It should be sent a week of ahead of the scheduled date.

- Make sure you always dry run your pitch. Find some outsiders to inspect the words and music of your pitch play. Listen to their reviews. Adjust, as always, recognizing there's no such thing as a perfect pitch.
- At the end of the day, remember that your investors want to know the following:
  o What—and how big and profitable—is the market you're targeting?
  o What's your big idea? Technology? Services? Hybrid? Is there any IP?
  o How many competitors are in the market now? How fast are new competitors entering the market?
  o How much money is required to launch? What's the expected monthly cash burn over the next 12 months?
  o What is your expected revenue and profitability over the next five years? (This, if course, is a wild-assed guess, a WAG, but necessary for the 9 AM investment committee meeting.) What you must do here is identify the drivers of rev-enue growth, at least as you understand them at the time of the pitch.
  o Who is the founder(s)? Who's on the management team?
  o What is their entrepreneurial history?
  o Are there any initial clients/customers?
- If you cannot answer these questions, you shouldn't even open your own checkbook, let alone ask anyone else for money.
- If you can show something, show it (rather than talk about it): there's no more powerful communication than sight, touch, smell and feel.

Funding and Valuation Takeaways

- If they cannot self-fund, entrepreneurs should seek disciplined Angels—also known as professional Angels—for funding. Again: not friends or family, despite the lore around the romance of friends and family gathering around their favorite entrepreneur to help make everyone who loves everybody wealthy. This is the very definition of naiveté: money will kill friendships and families, especially if the amount is large enough.

- If they cannot self-fund, entrepreneurs should start with disciplined Angels. Disciplined Angels understand risk. They're much more likely to endorse a strategic valuation methodology, though they also understand the tradeoff between early risk and strategic valuation, and therefore, because they're literally seeding the startup, deserve a good valuation, however *strategic* it might be.

- Entrepreneurs? Fund your company personally. If that's not possible or desirable, invite your founding team to invest, even small amounts. You might also require your founding Board of Directors to invest a nominal amount of money, such as $25K. The same deal can be extended to members of your founding Advisory Board.

- Self-funding avoids a valuation fight. You can set the valuation low and buy a lot of the company for relatively little money. You and your initial team can own nearly all the company from the initial seed round of financing. But self-funding is tricky.

- Entrepreneurs should never forget how to monetize their strategic importance: even when revenue and profits are exploding, they should never undersell their strategic value.

- Remember that institutional funding should only be pursued from positions of strength; same strategy applies to relationships with IBs.

- VCs are valuation crushers and will invariably try to apply the operational valuation methodology, no matter what the company really does.

- VCs will invariably apply the operational valuation methodology, no matter what the company really does. They do so because if you show up at a VC's office you probably need money, and the first desperation test entrepreneurs are given is their willingness to accept a low valuation. VCs administer this test because it protects the investment of their limited partners and, most importantly, themselves.
- *Never forget about the SBIR program for seed funding.*

Investment Term Sheet Takeaways

- What are they? The term sheet is the document that outlines the terms by which an investor (Angel or venture capital investor) will make a financial investment in your company. Term sheets tend to consist of three sections: funding, corporate governance and liquidation.
- Valuation lies at the core of term sheets presented by investors. It's a major part of every equity term sheet because it defines the percentage of equity the investors will own after an investment is made. There's always a *fight* about *pre-money* valuation—what your company is worth right now before an investment is made. Do you know? Have you developed a model that defends a specific valuation? Have you looked at comparable companies and their valuation metrics? (*Post-money* valuation defines valuation after the money has been invested in your company.)
- Pay very special attention to the option pool the investor defines. Pre-money option pools are often questioned by investors. Why is it so large? Or small? Everyone has a vested interest in the existence of an option pool to attract and reward employees. But the size and terms of the pool are always negotiated in the term sheet. Try to keep the option pool as is and prevent attempts to revalue the option pool after the transaction occurs, which will devalue the stock of the founders and early investors.

- Term sheets also define liquidation preferences—which is downside protection for the investors. Obviously, everyone hopes the company will do well, and there's tons of money falling from the sky to distribute, but if there's not, investors want to make sure they're in front of the line whenever money is handed out. This is where the pretty standard 1X liquidation preference kicks in, which simply means that the investors will get their money back before anyone else (like common shareholders) receives a dime.

- Watch out for participation rights, where the investors get the right to not only get their money back (the standard 1X liquidation preference) but also get to participate again in what's left after the initial distribution of funds. This is an attempt to double dip into the cash that's left after the first dip returns the initial capital investment: not good for entrepreneurs and common shareholders. So fight against participation rights (and dividends, which should be eliminated from seed and early-stage company term sheets).

- Should you—or any investors—expect antidilution protection? It's a reasonable request by seed-stage investors who buy preferred shares of your company. But realistically, it's protection against disaster—like when you must raise money at a valuation lower than the previous round (the dreaded *down round*). The only antidilution protection you should give is a weighted average one, where investors are required to invest additional capital in the event of a down round to *earn* the protection.

- After valuation, control is the most important feature of a term sheet, and control lies in the Board of Directors. Control of the board should correlate perfectly with ownership percentages, which is another reason why you must negotiate valuation as aggressively as possible. If investors own a third of your company, then the investor is entitled for one of three board seats. That said, nearly all corporate OAs require an independent director, though *i*ndependence is a relative term! While minority shareholders have a vote in the selection and approval of the independent board member, as minority shareholders—and likely new investors—they will generally not try to control the independent board member approval process. They will of course vet candidates, but by and large, the founders will manage the process. But when a larger investment is made and everyone is aligned with a growth strategy, board control will usually be expanded to include founders, investors, and independent Directors.

- Follow the money: if you accept $10M against a pre-money valuation of $40M, you need not share control of the company equally. But if you accept an investment of $20M on the same pre-money valuation, you will share control of the company, even though the postmoney valuation still gives you control. In that scenario, you and your principal investor would constitute a five-person board, where you have two seats, your investor has two, and there's a near-pure independent director. Or a seven-person board with the same distribution of seats: 3/3/1. Remember, however, the larger the board, the greater number of problems, simply because humans breed problems. Remember also that investments equal the ownership of categories of stock, such as preferred, common, and special. This is important because not all decisions are made by the Board of Directors. Some are made by shareholder vote.

- Investor rights is a quagmire. No one thinks about nailing down each other's rights when someone is dangling a shiny check with lots of zeros. But that's the only time investors and entrepreneurs may get the chance to have the discussion about what happens when things go wrong. Investors and entrepreneurs should expect bi-directional transparency, especially regarding debt, stock pools, benefits, or changes to the OA. But there are other areas where there might be considerable debate, such as access to the company's books, inspection of the company's IP, the right to external reviews and input around the selection of IBs, and other professionals. Many of these *rights* issues are difficult to discuss out of the context of specific scenarios.

But there are obviously many that require, for example, full inspection rights.

- As an entrepreneur, do you want your investors to be able to see everything you and the Board of Directors have done over the years? If not, why not? This is a triple-play question. It's a moral, ethical, and professional question. My advice to you is allow your investors to see whatever they want to see, simply because if you refuse them access, you are de facto guilty of hiding something, and why would you deliberately paint yourself into a corner of guilt? It makes no ethical, moral, or professional sense because you will forever display a tattoo on your forehead that repeats *"I never wanted my investors to see what I did with their money."*

Operating Agreement Takeaways

- Wikipedia helps with the basics: "An operating agreement is a key document ... because it outlines the business' financial and functional decisions including rules, regulations and provisions. The purpose of the document is to govern the internal operations of the business in a way that suits the specific needs of the business owners ... the operating agreement usually includes percentage of interests, allocation of profits and losses, member's rights and responsibilities and other provisions."
- OAs play different roles. At the very least, they are two-way protections. They define the way things operate and become the reference document of record—and dispute. Without an OA, everyone's at risk.
- The issue of inspection rights—like investor rights in a term sheet—is one of the most important aspects of an OA. You and your investors should share transparency as a mutual goal. But many of the disputes among members of an LLC are often about inspection rights.
- Remember that regardless of how specific the OA is, there will be challenges. This is is where larger issues of integrity and

professionalism drive the dispute process. If an investor wants to see the books or inspect board meeting minutes, and the entrepreneur—perhaps you—tells them they cannot inspect the books or review board minutes, what's the message? Clearly, if an entrepreneur (hopefully, not you) refuses to grant access to corporate records, there's a larger problem that can be summarized in a single, simple question: *why?* There's no argument an entrepreneur can make that justifies hiding the books from investors—unless there's something the entrepreneur (hopefully, not you) wants to hide.

- Investors should have their attorneys make certain that the OAs they sign make it damn near impossible for management and the board to hide records from investors. But you must assume —sadly, but realistically—that if there's something to hide, the people in charge—and their paid legal hench-men (and women) —will try to hide it from the investors. Digital entrepreneurs and their investors must fight for the rights to which they're entitled—or the start-up process will derail.

Buzz Takeaways

- Pay (early and often) for buzz: dedicate significant resources to marketing and PR, and never DIY.
- Creatively engineer buzz always informed by empirical market research—not anecdotes about what might sell.
- Learn about what buzz works (and what doesn't) from successful companies in your domain—and copy them.
- Remember that buzz today (and forever) is more digital than traditional, so exploit all the digital channels.
- Do not buzz a whole new category alone: you will almost certainly fail.
- GenAI is your buzz friend, not just for buzz and all things marketing, but across the board.

Teams Takeaway

- You cannot start an innovative company by yourself. Remember, you are the company you keep. Startups need a combination of professionals who are broad and deep. Some will know a lot about a little about PR, technology, or finance, and some will know a little about everything. The latter are your glue; the former are your arms and legs. Understand the difference.

Building and Growing Takeaways

- Make sure you understand the financial markets at the time of your launch. The markets will define your prospects for funding as your company grows, exit opportunities, and customer abilities to buy your products and services. Once you have a read on the market, adjust your strategy and tactics accordingly—but try to resist leaving the planet to do so.
- Make sure there's substance to your business model. Digital entrepreneurs should stay grounded, while opportunistic.
- Services companies (perhaps like yours) evolve over time. Messaging is always important, but delivery is necessary and sufficient for survival. Evolve over time—and quickly. Seek feedback from the marketplace and industry experts with no vested interests in your company. Test repositioning messages continuously. Watch your market and your customers. Talk to them.
- Scheduled, programmed incubation is a tough business despite how codified incubation *methodology* is. The very idea of incubation and the appeal of prolific incubators is sometimes hard to resist, especially by investors looking for more action than their usual deal flow generates. But the track record of incubation is mixed at best, and according to research, poor. So, be careful not to be seduced by *incupreteurs* who promise the moon for some money, and then a little more money and then a ton more.

Marketing and PR Takeaways

- Some entrepreneurs fear the process (and worry about the outcomes) because they've only experienced digital marketing as customers, not as creators. Their knowledge about the process, methods, and tools is shallow. If your knowledge about digital marketing and PR is limited, learn a lot and search for more. You cannot go slowly here, but at the same time, you don't need a full-time Chief Marketing Officer (CMO) either. The fractional help of an expert is what you need to launch.
- Most companies also change their message and their content way too frequently. Because the messaging and content creation tools make it easy to modify everything, many entrepreneurs cannot resist the temptation to make changes day after day.
- Startups need to go to market with a message that resonates with customers, and while that message should evolve over time, it's smarter to take a little more time to hone the message (and supporting content) than to release too early, only to have to quickly modify your identity shortly after you launch. Take the time to get the message as *right* as you can, recognizing that over time you will have to modify your market identity. You don't want to make changes every week.
- ***Leverage GenAI marketing tools every which way you can.***

Sales Takeaways

- Find salespersons with deep subject matter expertise. If you're selling analytics products or services, your salespersons should know a ton about analytics and the business domains to which they're selling. If they don't, replace them.
- Performance matters more than words. Brutally track actual sales performance, not the elegance of promises or rigged benchmarking exercises.
- I am a huge fan of giving away products and services to establish sales beach heads. While this is an expensive strategy, it immediately gets your products and services into the

marketplace. I gave away services early in my company's growth stage all the time. I also over-delivered—all the time—and made sure that my (paying) clients knew exactly what they were getting for free. We would routinely build storyboards of user requirements as loss-leaders to the kind of engagements we desperately wanted—and needed to survive.

- To make money, you must spend money. Yes, an old axiom, but a tough one for startups to practice. Products are easier to give away than services, because they're generally hosted in the cloud where accounts can be set up for 30 days or so to allow prospective customers to play with what you've developed. If they like it, they will buy it; if they don't, they can help you understand why they didn't buy it. Value no matter what the outcome.

- If your products and services are content-related, it's especially easy to share them with prospective clients. If your products are complicated software platforms, for example, then the cost of sharing is high, because you will have to train and support the trial if you want them to ultimately buy your product. All expensive, but all necessary.

- Selling as early as possible makes sense, though be careful not to oversell with an eager customer who wants your product or service tomorrow. Customer knowledge is always essential, but the best advice is to never pretend to be a large enterprise. Start-up–customer relationship management is unique and should be managed accordingly. Expectations are appropriately different and can lead to long-term relationships—if you execute your first engagements well.

- Customer intimacy is much easier to achieve as a startup than as a large vendor selling just one more account. Sell intimacy—while you're still small.

- At the end of the day, sales processes should be formal, repeatable, and adaptive.

- Remember that start-up selling is experimental. You won't know what works until it works. Test and measure different processes, scrips, and value propositions—and different salespersons.
- While you (as the CEO) may be wonderful (or not), you need to determine who on the team is also effective interacting with customers—and who's not.

Finance Takeaways

- Startups should initially allocate most of their funds to product/service development and people. Once they launch, the ratio should balance to sales, marketing, and delivery to lighthouse customers with long digital reaches—even if that means some product/service features go undeveloped.
- Entrepreneurs must make sure that finances are well organized, well documented, and transparent with the help of part-time financial professionals with deep experience with startups. They should focus constantly on cash flow, burn rates, and runway. They should describe Plan B fundraising scenarios.

Structure Takeaways

- Because you are small, elaborate, hierarchical organizational structures make no sense. We can quickly dismiss the functional and divisional structures. They're too complicated and assume lots of people—and you definitely don't have lots of people.

- Startups can benefit from a matrix organization structure influenced by aspects of the project/case/team/flat/virtual organizational structures. In practice, this means that responsibility is shared across projects by teams living in a loose corporate matrix.
- Just about everything you and your team do to run the business has been incarnated in software. Digital marketing, CRM, financial reporting, expense reporting, email campaigning, project management, analytics, team communications, and

training, among many other tasks, activities, and functions are all available to digital entrepreneurs and their teams. Find and deploy. You can organize and manage yourself and your company with inexpensive business software.

Incentives Takeaways

- You must decide how to incentivize and reward your founding team with shares in your company. There are at least two ways to do this. The first way is to award preferred shares of the NewCo (new company) to key members of the team. The second is to grant common shares or options to purchase common shares. Preferred share grants are the best gift you can give employees. Common shares are OK but not nearly as good as preferred shares. Options are the least generous because they must be earned over time.

- There are multiple classes of stock in a company. You need a philosophy and an attorney to map the strengths and weaknesses of each class. My philosophy is on the generous side. You can decide for yourself, but if you want to motivate your team give them a meaningful piece of the company.

Exit Takeaways

- Make sure you're aware of the exit *zones*.

The Dead Zone

- Worst exit: bankruptcy. Remember that it's more likely you will lose everything than become rich, so when that day arrives, accept it professionally and ethically if you can (and not all entrepreneurs can).

- Horrible exit: *acqui-hire,* where your team is sold to the highest bidder for pennies on the dollar. Sometimes this is the best you can do. Your products and services may have failed, but your team is solid—and therefore desirable, especially if their skills are in white-hot technology areas. Acquirers will offer you money and stock for these people.

The Near-Dead Zone

- Weak exit: an IP-only sale, where your pending IP is sold to the highest bidder for a negotiated (OK) operational or (better) strategic value. This is also a less than ideal outcome for you and your investors, but at least there's something for everyone to sell.

The Comfort Zone

- Solid exit: recapitalization, where your company is purchased by outside investors at a negotiated value that results in a buyout for the founders and Angel investors at some multiple of the initial valuation of the company.

- Good exit: lifestyle-cash-extraction, where management and investors suck as much cash as they can—for as long as they can—from a successful ongoing business. This *good* exit is not a real exit, but the realization that the business may be a cash cow capable of yielding milk every quarter.

The End Zone

- Excellent exit: strategic acquisition by a company that believes your business (revenue and customers) adds financial and (ideally) strategic value to their existing portfolio of products and services. This is your goal, especially if the valuation is strategic.
- Best exit: an IPO, where shares of your company are sold to institutions and the public. While this exit is a dream for many entrepreneurs, it essentially represents the sale of your company to strangers will be bet on your future.

Final Thoughts

So how can you avoid bad exit zones?

- First, rid yourself of start-up myths. While it's obviously exciting to pursue one's dreams, dreams should be brutally tempered with reality. Think about what's possible, not what's likely, but possible. Manage your expectations—and the expectations of your investors.

- You must understand the technology world you're entering and the market your solution will address. Really, you must understand technology trends and consumer and business markets—as well as what your competitors are doing.

- You also need to understand the whole start-up process—which is often twisted by *players* with conflicting agendas. As you build and grow your startup, pay attention to business basics, and organize your team as matrixed project managers. Make sure you let the world know you exist with every digital tool in the box.

- Learn about alternative valuation methods and models. Learn about deal terms and by all means take some time with your Operating Agreement—OA—and encourage your investors to do the same. Don't plant landmines in your OA designed to kill investors who ask perfectly reasonable business questions about the state of your (and their) startup. Do not take money from friends or dumb Angels unless you're prepared for the relationships to die.

- Be transparent, please. Never hide things from your team, your investors, or your customers. Keep your necessary evils—VCs, lawyers, and IBs—at arms length, but manage them very closely. (A contradiction that must be managed.)

- Know when you're good, bad, and dying. When you're good, proceed cautiously. When you're bad, correct quickly and decisively. When you're dying, accept it gracefully, and do whatever you can to ease the pain of your team, your investors, and your customers—the stakeholders who took the journey with you, the journey that unfortunately ended badly. Your personal and professional reputation will be defined by how you handle failure (much more than how you handle success).

- Along the way, you need to carry a small mirror you can use to assess who you are, what you know, how you're perceived, and how you organize and manage your startup. Look at it often and invite some objective professionals—not friends—to tell you what they see.
- Finally, there's one principle that's undeniable. It's the one you should apply to your entire professional life: follow the money.

How about the landmines that should be avoided? Or the reasons why entrepreneurs fail? Here are 10:

1. *Not Smart Enough*

I'm not talking about IQ here. Entrepreneurial IQ (EIQ) is about holistic understanding of situations. Many entrepreneurs understand their idea, but not the market that will accept or reject the idea. Nor do they understand how accidental, uncontrollable, unscheduled innovation actually works. Or who the real competitors are. Often, entrepreneurs have too little domain depth: they literally do not know what they're talking about (though they often talk a good game). Many entrepreneurs fail because they're not actually entrepreneurs but some variation on the theme. Even worse are entrepreneurs who believe they're terrific at activities at which everyone else believes they're horrible. If an entrepreneur is incapable of seeing what everyone else sees, he or she is blind to success.

2. *Not Knowing Who's Who*

Entrepreneurs often fail because they cannot separate friends from enemies. They cannot identify EIQ from fluff or bluff. They cannot find a good part-time accountant, and they have no idea how to assess the skills and experience of legal counsel. They also fail because they cannot recognize smart loyal co-founders and employees or how to optimize their contributions. They fail because they cannot separate dumb Angel investors from disciplined ones. There's a lot to know, and many entrepreneurs just don't know enough about the players.

3. *Not Finding Enough of the Right Kind of Funding*

Entrepreneurs often fail because they cannot raise the right kind of funding at the right time at the right valuation. They use too much of their own money and way too much money from friends and family—which becomes a distraction every time a friend or family member asks about how the company—and their investment—is doing. Entrepreneurs fail because they don't know how to value their company or phase investments along timelines designed to optimize valuations. They fail to appreciate how much money it takes to meet milestones. Or how to respect their investors who deserve professional communications on a regular basis—especially if they plan to keep asking them for money.

4. *Grandiose Expectations*

While it's sometimes good to believe in miracles, it's no way to run a startup. Entrepreneurs who fail often do so because they believe they will change the world, and if the world doesn't welcome their authority, it's the world's fault, not theirs. Entrepreneurs fail because they're often self-delusional and greedy believing that they're just a sale away from revolutionizing an industry and becoming filthy rich.

5. *Horrible Soft Skills*

Entrepreneurs often fail because they're not housebroken, because they speak their minds no matter how inappropriate or inopportune the situation may be. Some entrepreneurs are famously outspoken and controversial—we know who they are—but they generally became that way *after* their first hit startup. If an entrepreneur cannot listen, is insecure, short-tempered, and intolerant of opposing opinions, he or she will fail. The worst entrepreneurs are the ones who cannot accept responsibility for anyone and spend their days and nights looking for someone—anyone—to blame for their mistakes.

6. *Bad Partners*

Entrepreneurs often fail because they hang out with the wrong people. *Wrong* here is a broad term. It includes colleagues who agree with everything the entrepreneur says, *good guys* who others endorse but are unfamiliar to the entrepreneur, channel partners who use the entrepreneur to channel their own sales, legal counsel that racks up unnecessary fees, and gurus who know just about everything about anything. Good entrepreneurs have a purpose filter through which they spend their time.

7. *Wrong Sales*

Entrepreneurs often fail because they cannot sell to the right clients at the right time for the right price. Start-up sales are obviously fundamentally different from the sales that established companies enjoy on an almost automatic pace. Good entrepreneurs understand all forms and flavors of lighthouse sales processes, logo hunting, how to buy the right early customers. Entrepreneurs who fail shortchange sales in favor of competing activities, especially R&D.

8. *Market Invisibility*

Entrepreneurs often fail because their companies are invisible to the world because they cannot bear to spend money on marketing and PR. This is a huge mistake that some entrepreneurs make when the money gets tight. Polishing products and services until they shine brightly in the sunshine is a waste of money. Smart entrepreneurs get the word out early and often via all available media, especially digital media: *if they cannot find you, they cannot buy you.*

9. *Pivot Paralysis*

Entrepreneurs often fail because they cannot adapt to unpredictable events and conditions (as if any entrepreneurial events or conditions are predictable). All startups require pivots. Unsuccessful entrepreneurs cannot pivot. Instead, they stay their own courses—even when the entire world believes they're severely off course and about to crash into the side of a large mountain.

10. *No Sense of the Inevitable Exit*

Entrepreneurs often fail because they cannot gauge their ultimate exit relatively early in their journey. Call it instinct or judgment, the range of exit outcomes begins to reveal itself once the products and services hit the market and once the source and pace of competition clarifies. Is the exit an IPO or an acquisition? Is it an acqui-hire or a recapitalization? Good entrepreneurs have a sense of how an exit will occur (if one occurs at all) within a year of their launch. Bad ones believe in miracles.

In the beginning of this book, I asked you if you had the stomach for entrepreneurialism. I asked you to look in the mirror every day. If you can make tough decisions. If you can fire your friends. If you can tell white lies—and maybe even some really black ones. If you can work on three hours sleep. If you can skip family outings. If you can travel at a moment's notice. If you can resist sex at the office. If you can avoid drugs and alcohol. Can you do all these things?

Look, starting and growing a company is hard, complicated work. There's so much to learn, know, and do. The ground below your feet shifts every day. On Monday, everyone's your friend, but on Tuesday, everyone hates you. By Friday, you have all new friends—one of which is always named chaos. You know that the probability of success is low. But in spite of the odds, you're willing to take a shot at achieving something very few professionals ever achieve.

This book provides some guidance about how to navigate through the maze of people, processes, technologies, and markets that together provide an opportunity to beat the odds. It's tough in places—sometimes steeped in negative experiences. But it's organized that way for what should be obvious reasons. None of this is easy. But you already know that.

So that's it.

Have fun on your journey to fabulous wealth—however challenging it might be.

Call me if you'd like to talk.

References

Acar, O. 2024. "Is Your AI-First Strategy Causing More Problems Than It's Solving?" *Harvard Business Review*, March.

Agile Alliance. 2024. "What Is Minimum Viable Product (MVP)?"

Alden, W. 2014. "Venture Capital Firm Settles S.E.C. Charges Over 'Pay-to-Play.'" *The New York Times*, June.

Andriole, S. 2023. "Five Ways Executives Misunderstand Technology." *Communications of the ACM*, December.

Andriole, S. 2015. "Why Innovation Almost Always Fails." *Forbes Magazine*, February.

Andriole, S.J. 1976. "Progress Report on the Development of an Integrated Crisis Warning System." Technical Report 76–19. McLean, VA: Decisions and Designs, Inc.

Arribas, L. 2022. "The Corporate Venture Comeback: What Startups Considering CVC Need to Know." *Mercury*, April.

Andriole, S. 1997. "Requirements-Driven ALN Course Design, Development, Delivery & Evaluation." *Online Learning*, 1 (2).

Bass, A. 2003. "Integration Management—Cigna's Self-Inflicted Wounds." *CIO Magazine,* March.

Bendix, J. 2023. "Cigna Using AI to Reject Claims, Lawsuit Charges." *Medical Economics*, August.

Brown, S. 2022. "8 Apps for a More Eco-Friendly Sustainable Life." *CNET*, April.

Caldbeck, R. 2014. "7 Questions for Your Investment Banker." *Entrepreneur*, September.

Cote, C. 2023. "Startup Incubators Vs. Accelerator: Which One Is Right for You?" *Harvard Business School Online*, August.

CustomGPT.ai. 2024. "CustomGPT.ai for Education: Engaging Students and Delivering Dynamic Learning With an AI Course Assistant." *CustomGPT.ai.*

Davis, O. 2015. "What Is the Carried Interest Tax Loophole." *International Business Times*, June.

De Cremer, D., and G. Kasparov. 2021. "AI Should Augment Human Intelligence, Not Replace It." *Harvard Business Review*, March.

Dhir, R. 2022. "Compiled vs. Certified Financial Statements: What's the Difference?" *Investopedia*, March.

Dickler, J. 2022. "Verdict in Fraud Case of Theranos Founder Elizabeth Holmes Offers Lessons for Investors." *CNBC*, January.

Edison Investment Research. 2008. "XL TechGroup, Inc." *Edison Investment Research*, March.

FasterCapital. 2024. "Participation Rights: What Are They and How do They Impact Your Equity Funding." *FasterCapital,* June.

Fetsch, E. 2015. "Are Incubators Beneficial to Emerging Businesses?" *The Kauffman Foundation*, March.

Frawley, A. 2024. "63 of the Best Marketing Tools for Startups." *StartupGRIND*.

Galloway, S. 2022. "Tell Me a Story." *No Mercy/No Malice*, January.

Gowder, C. 2023. "Recent Research: Impacts of Accelerators and Incubators on Economic Development." *SSTI*, April.

Guest Author. 2010. "Top 10 Reasons Why Entrepreneurs Hate lawyers." *Venture Hacks*, January.

Guinness, H. 2024. "The Best AI Image Generators in 2024." *Zapier*.

Harkness, L., K. Robinson, E. Stein, and W. Wu. 2023. "How Generative AI Can Boost Consumer Marketing." *McKinsey*, December.

Hayes, A. 2024. "What Is a Simple Agreement for Future Equity (SAFE)." *Investopedia*, January.

IBISWorld. 2024. "Industries With the Highest Profit Margin in the US in 2024." *IBISWorld*.

Kagan, J. 2024. "Investment Banker: What They Do, Required Skills, and Examples." *Investopedia*, March.

Kenton, W. 2020. "Commercialization: Definition, Plus the Product Rollout Process." *Investopedia*, December.

Key, P. 2001. "Tech Meltdown Isn't Safeguard's Only Woe." *Philadelphia Business Journal*, January.

Lakhani, K. 2023. "AI Won't Replace Humans—But Humans With AI Will Replace Humans Without AI." *Harvard Business Review*, August.

Lasica, J.D. and Bale, K. (2011). Top 20 Social Media Monitoring Vendors for Business. *Social Media Listening*, January.

Laurie, D. 2001. *Venture Catalyst: The Five Strategies For Explosive Corporate Growth.* Nicholas Brealey Publishing.

Levy, S. 2021. "AR Is Where the Real Metaverse Is Going to Happen." *Wired Magazine,* November.

MaRS. 2024. "Elements of a Term Sheet: Funding, Liquidation and Corporate Governance." *MaRS Start-Up Tool Kit*.

Martela, F., and J. Luoma. 2021. "Why AI Will Never Replace Managers." *Harvard Business Review*, September.

Mayadas, F. 1997. "Asynchronous Learning Networks: A Sloan Foundation Perspective." *Journal of Asynchronous Learning Networks* 1 (1).

McCombie, III, D. 2022. "The ROI of Hiring an Investment Banker." *Forbes Magazine*, November.

Milburn, R. 2015. "Private Equity: Beware of Zombie Funds." *PENTA*, August.

Miller, D. 2015. "8 Digital-Marketing Tips for Bootstrapped." *Entrepreneur*, March.

Moran, S. 2023. "Artificial Intelligence at Cigna—Four Use Cases." *Emerj*, August.

Mulcahy, D. 2013. "Six Myths About Venture Capitalists." *Harvard Business Review*, May.

O'Brien, P. 2024. "Why Accelerators Fail Startup Founders." *LinkedIn*, April.

O'Connell, B. and B. Curry. 2022. "What Are Angel Investors?" *Forbes Advisor*, July.

Parrish, M. 2024. "Five Years After Closing the Shire Deal, Takeda Is Ready to Harvest From Its Latest Reinvention." *PharmaVoice*, Janaury.

Piercy, W. 2010. "You Want to See My What?!?: An Owner's Right to Inspect Business Records." *BFV*, June.

Primack, D. 2014. "How a Zombie VC Firm Broke Pay-to-Play Rules." *Fortune Magazine*, June.

Rao, D. 2023. "20 VCs Capture 95% of VC Profits: Implications For Entrepreneurs & Venture Ecosystems." *Forbes Magazine*.

Roos, D. 2021. "Top 5 Myths About Microsoft." *How Stuff Works*.

Sag, A. 2021. "Why Microsoft Won The $22 Billion Army HoloLens 2 AR Deal." *Forbes Magazine*, April.

Sell, C. 2024. "Generative AI in Marketing." *GrowthLoop*, February.

Senz, K. 2023. "Is AI Coming for Your Job?" *Harvard Business Review Notes*, April.

SHAREWORKS. 2023. "Term Sheets: The Definitive Guide for Entrepreneurs." *SHAREWORKS Founder Handbook,* November.

Shrier, D., J. Emanuel, and M. Harris. 2023. "Is Your Job AI Resilient?" *Harvard Business Review*, October.

Stripe. 2023. "How to Issue Stock to Founders: What Early Startups Need to Know." *Stripe,* November.

Thomson Reuters. 2024. "Simple Agreement for Future Equity (SAFE)." *Thomson-Reuters Practice Law.*

TRUiC Team. 2024. "21 Top Venture Capital Firms (2024)." *TRUiC*, January.

Tsosie, C., A. Rosenberg, and L. Anthony. 2023. "19 Best Small-Business Apps of May 2024." *Nerdwallet*, October.

US Securities & Exchange Commission. 2024. "What Different Types of Securities Are Issued to Startup Investors?" *US Securities & Exchange Commission.*

Vallance, C. 2023. "AI Could Replace Equivalent of 300 Million Jobs—Report." *BBC*, March.

Warner, M. 2001. "Pete Musser Built His Company Over 40 Years. Then He Was Seduced by the Internet." *Fortune Magazine*, March.

Workfully. 2024. "12 Reasons Why Early Stage Startups Should Hire Fractional Leaders." *LinkedIn*, February.

Zapflow. 2023. "How Much Should You Know About the Technology You Invest In?" *Zapflow*.

About the Author

Steve Andriole was in the room for the cases described in **Start-Ups DECLASSIFIED.** He has started and exited several companies. He worked as a venture capitalist and was involved in 12 initial public offerings (IPOs). He is an active Angel investor. He has sat on many start-up boards.

He was the Director of the Cybernetics Technology Office of the Defense Advanced Research Projects Agency (DARPA). He was also the Senior Vice President (SVP) and Chief Technology Officer (CTO) at Cigna Corporation, the Interim Chief Information Officer (CIO) at Shire Pharmaceuticals, the SVP and CTO at Safeguard Scientifics, a Principal at TL Ventures, and the founder or cofounder of four companies.

He has worked closely with many companies at all stages of their development and was the primary Wall Street contact for Safeguard, frequently interacting with the analysts that covered Safeguard and the start-ups it founded. He participated directly in raising over $1B for startups.

He is currently the Thomas G. Labrecque Professor of Business Technology in the Villanova School of Business at Villanova University where he teaches artificial intelligence, emerging business technologies, and business-technology strategy. He is formerly a Professor of Information Systems and Electrical and Computer Engineering at Drexel University in Philadelphia, Pennsylvania, and a Professor (and Chairman) of the Department of Information Systems and Systems Engineering at George Mason University where he held the George Mason Institute Professorship of Information Technology. He is the author of several recently published books, including *The Digital Playbook: How to Win the Strategic Technology Game*, Pearson/Financial Times, 2023, and *The Innovator's Imperative: Rapid Technology Adoption for Digital Transformation*, coauthor, Taylor Francis Group/CRC Press, 2017. He has published articles in the *Sloan Management Review*, the *Communications of the ACM*, the *Communications of the AIS,* and *IEEE IT Professional*, among many other journals. He was a regular contributor to *Forbes Magazine* where he published over 30 articles on innovation, entrepreneurialism, and startups.

Index

www.ingramcontent.com/pod-product-compliance
Lightning Source LLC
Chambersburg PA
CBHW061200220326
41599CB00025B/4548